The
OUTDOOR
POTTED
BULB

NEW APPROACHES TO
CONTAINER GARDENING WITH
FLOWERING BULBS

ROB PROCTOR

Photographs by Lauren Springer
and Rob Proctor
with watercolors by the author

FOREWORD BY JOHN E. BRYAN

SIMON & SCHUSTER

New York London Toronto Sydney Tokyo Singapore

For Steve,
who couldn't be a
better friend

SIMON & SCHUSTER
Simon & Schuster Building
Rockefeller Center
1230 Avenue of the Americas
New York, NY 10020

Edited by Charles A. de Kay
Designed by Jan Melchior
Typesetting by Cast of Characters, Hillsdale, N.J.
Printed in Singapore

10 9 8 7 6 5 4 3 2 1

Library of Congress Cataloging in Publication Data
Proctor, Rob.
The Outdoor potted bulb / Rob Proctor ; photographs by Lauren Springer ;
watercolors and supplemental photography by the author ; foreword by John E. Bryan.
p.   cm.
Includes bibliographical references and index.
ISBN 0-671-87034-3
1. Bulbs 2. Plants, Potted. 3. Container gardening I. Title
SB425.P76 1993
635.9'44–dc20   93-6664
                                 CIP

ACKNOWLEDGMENTS

Making a book takes more than just a handful of people. Lauren and I thank our generous friends from across the country who shared their experiences with us and allowed us to photograph in their gardens and homes. Our special gratitude goes to Tom Peace for his invaluable contribution.

OUR THANKS TO:

Kent Choiniere and Zachary Cox
Mary Ellen Tonsing
Angela Overy
Susan Sheridan
John and Marilyn Massey
Lyn Martin
Nancy and Jack Riley
Ken Hamblin and Sue Hoover
Kathy and Steve Meyer
Norma Hazen

Tish Hazard
Jane Lappin
Judy and Jerry Licht
Four Mile Historic Park,
    Denver, Colorado
Green Acres Nursery, Golden, Colorado
Chanticleer, Wayne, Pennsylvania
Montrose Nursery,
    Hillsborough, North Carolina

Denver Botanic Gardens,
    Denver, Colorado
Longwood Gardens, Kennett Square,
    Pennsylvania
Paulino Gardens, Denver, Colorado
Roger's Gardens,
    Corona del Mar, California
Jos. A. Hren Nurseries,
    Amagansett, New York

SPECIAL THANKS TO:

Tom and Diane Peace
Ray Daugherty
Kelly Grummons
Robin Preston
Starr Tapp
David Macke
Michael Pavsek
Corinne Levy and Tom Segal
Mary Kay Long and Dennis Unites
Jane Taylor
Rosalie Isom
Leslie Knill
Solange Gignac and Susan Eubank of
    The Helen Fowler Library, Denver
    Botanic Gardens, Denver, Colorado

Barbara Pitschel of The Helen Crocker
    Library of Horticulture at Strybing
    Arboretum, San Francisco, California
Brent Heath, The Daffodil Mart,
    Gloucester, Virginia
Betsy Gullan,
    Pennsylvania Horticultural Society
Kay Hall, Happy Canyon Flowers,
    Denver, Colorado
Keith Funk and Dot Pollack,
    Echter's Greenhouse and Garden
    Center, Arvada, Colorado
Steve Houck and Jung So,
    Accent Gardens, Boulder, Colorado
Phil Miller and Jeff Level, Roger's
    Gardens, Corona del Mar, California

BJ Dyer, Bouquets, Denver, Colorado
Robert Herald, Colvin Randall, and
    Julie Padrutt, Longwood Gardens,
    Kennett Square, Pennsylvania
Tovah Martin, Logee's Greenhouse,
    Danielson, Connecticut
Christopher Woods, Chanticleer,
    Wayne, Pennsylvania
Nancy Goodwin and Doug Ruhren,
    Montrose Nursery, Hillborough,
    North Carolina
Sherman Library and Gardens,
    Corona del Mar, California
Hotel St. Maarten, Laguna Beach,
    California

All photographs by Lauren Springer and Rob Proctor, except:
pg. 94 Judy Glattstein, pg. 93 Saxon Holt, pg. 116 Mary Ellen Tonsing, pg. 116 Netherland Flower Bulb Information Center, pg. 15 John Bryan

CONTENTS

CHAPTER TWO
A SUMMER SHOW
38

Achimenes (nut orchid) ◆ Acidanthera (Abyssinian gladiolus) ◆ Agapanthus (lily-of-the-Nile) ◆ Allium (ornamental onion) Alstroemeria (Peruvian lily) ◆ X Amarcrinum (crinodonna lily) ◆ Amaryllis (belladonna lily) ◆ Anigozanthos (kangaroo paw) ◆ Arisaema (jack-in-the-pulpit) ◆ Begonia (tuberous begonia) ◆ Belamcanda (blackberry lily) ◆ Caladium (angel wings) ◆ Canna (Indian shot) ◆ Colchicum (meadow saffron) ◆ Colocasia (elephant ear) ◆ Crinum (milk-and-wine-lily) ◆ Crocosmia (coppertip, montbretia) ◆ Crocus (autumn-flowering crocus) ◆ Curcuma (hidden lily) ◆ Dahlia ◆ Dicentra (bleeding heart) ◆ Dietes (wild iris) ◆ Erythronium (trout lily) ◆ Eucomis (pineapple lily) ◆ Galtonia (summer hyacinth) ◆ Gladiolus (spear lily) ◆ Haemanthus (paint brush) ◆ Hedychium (ginger lily) ◆ Hemerocallis (daylily) ◆ Hymenocallis (Peruvian daffodil) ◆ Ipomoea (sweet-potato vine) ◆ Liatris (gayfeather) ◆ Lilium (lily) ◆ Lycoris (magic lily) ◆ Neomarica (apostle plant, twelve apostles) ◆ Nerine (Guernsey lily) ◆ Ornithogalum (chincherinchee) ◆ Oxalis (wood sorrel) ◆ Polianthes (tuberose) ◆ Sauromatum (voodoo lily) ◆ Sprekelia (Aztec lily) ◆ Sternbergia (golden chalice) ◆ Tigridia (Mexican shell-flower) ◆ Tulbaghia (society garlic) ◆ Zantedeschia (summer calla lily) ◆ Zephyranthes (zephyr lily)

FOREWORD

It is with the greatest of pleasure that I write this foreword. Bulbs are, after all, my favorite plants. When I first read the manuscript I had to admit that the author had indeed found an aspect of bulb growing that needed attention —where else will you find such concise details of growing bulbs in pots?—but with this book this is no longer the case.

Much has been written about bulbs. Much still needs to be written. Rob Proctor has, with this work, filled a need; he has written entertainingly and the book contributes to our knowledge of these marvels of nature. Perhaps more importantly, it will encourage gardeners, even if they have no garden, to try their hand at growing bulbs, and certainly will increase their appreciation of bulbs.

We should not be surprised. Our libraries are enriched by his works. In the "Antique Flower" series we enjoy the combination of good, sound, and practical writing. In *The Outdoor Potted Bulb* we have more sound writing, combined with an obvious appreciation of art in the photographs and artistic adornments, perhaps not a surprise as the author is himself an accomplished artist. His keen eye for detail and his love of all plants are evident throughout the book.

There is no greater gift an author can give than to convey, in well chosen words, the essential knowledge which has been derived from experience.

Some might wish to discuss why, in a book about growing bulbs in pots, *Colocasia*, *Liatris*, and *Anigozanthos* are included. Perhaps the question should be why these genera have not been discussed in other works on bulbs!

When humor, much in evidence here, appreciation of art, practical knowledge, and imagination are combined, you have a combination that is hard—if not impossible—to beat. It is indeed fortunate for all of us who live with plants that Rob Proctor decided to give his attention and devote his many skills to growing bulbs in pots. Armed with the information contained herein, readers will surely be challenged to grow more, and be able to proceed with confidence. Surely I would never be one to discourage that, I would be robbing people of the pleasures of growing bulbs.

Just what are these contributions to our knowledge? For one, we have practical instructions disguised in charming prose. For another, we have colorful suggestions for plant combinations, not forcefully expressed but subtly conveyed by pleasing photographs. We have charts and lists that are straightforward and easy to understand. Rob Proctor tells stories that link the plants with their history, so that, when you hold a bulb in the palm of your hand, you can appreciate its connection with the past as you anticipate the unfurling of the beauty that, with the passage of time, will be yours to enjoy.

Read on keen gardener. You are embarking on a pleasant journey. Your knowledge—and, without a doubt, your appreciation of the plant world—is about to be increased. You will be the richer for the experience.

WHILE GARDENERS IN TEMPERATE CLIMATES GROW CYCLAMENS ON THE WINDOWSILL, CALIFORNIANS DISPLAY THEM OUTSIDE.

John E. Bryan
Sausalito, California

INTRODUCTION

AUSPICIOUS BEGINNINGS

Growing bulbs in containers for summer display is an old custom that blossomed during the Victorian era. Then, as now, horticulture was a hot topic, and the fires of discovery were stoked by new species of exotica discovered by plant hunters, which were flowing into England and the United States. A passion for horticulture, then, was an integral part in a larger fascination with the all of the natural sciences. The more exotic, the better, so that all things tropical held a special appeal to Victorian gardeners, who put botanists on a pedestal and plants in fancy urns.

A wealth of tropical and subtropical plants—from *Achimenes* to *Zantedeschia*—brought from the farthest reaches of the globe found favor, and potted bulbous plants soon adorned the porch, terrace, and conservatory. Cannas, caladiums, and colocasias became fashionable focal points. Some bulbs were passing fads, and would be difficult to locate today, but others took their place in the legacy of one of the most exciting periods of horticulture.

The passing of the Victorian era doomed some plants to horticultural banishment from refined circles. The beloved hyacinth and other favorites became old-fashioned overnight. Catalogues gradually dropped these old favorites, which were relegated to cottage gardens and unfashionable windowsills. Dust collected on the pages of Victoriana.

TEXTURES OF TERRA COTTA, FLAGSTONE, AND VINTAGE VICTORIAN LEATHER COMPLEMENT THE FASCINATING HOODED FLOWERS OF JACK-IN-THE-PULPIT.

UNASSAILABLE ADVANTAGES

Some of the most beautiful plants of summer are bulbs that are most easily grown in pots. But just what makes potted bulbs so special for the gardener today? Just as container gardening usually evokes more than just a windowbox of geraniums, potted bulbs offer boundless opportunities for creative gardening beyond the container of tulips on the winter windowsill. They come in all shapes and sizes, offering exquisite blossoms and extraordinary foliage. Adaptable and relatively easy to grow, potted bulbs return great beauty for a small investment of time and money.

With potted bulbs alone, it is possible to arrange to have flowers in every free spot in the house and garden during each month of the year. Many gardeners rely on pots of spring-blooming bulbs like crocus, daffodils, and tulips or tender paperwhites and amaryllis to keep up their flagging spirits in winter. These bulbs for off-season indoor pleasure are featured in the companion volume, *The Indoor Potted Bulb*, which explores the options of the indoor bulb garden. Then the trees leaf out, the garden comes back to life, and bulbs are largely forgotten by most gardeners, yet the possibilities have just begun.

Every garden, no matter what the region or climate may be, offers tremendous opportunities to enjoy

BOLD LEAVES OF POTTED CANNA **'WYOMING'**
ARCH OVER FUCHSIA **'GARTEN-MEISTER**
BONSTEDT' AND SCENTED GERANIUMS.

potted bulbs. From a city rooftop or balcony to a spacious terrace or veranda, brimming containers of bulbs add color, grace and excitement to the scene. Sun-drenched terraces, shady arbors and gazebos, secluded courtyards, and multi-purpose porches and decks all make perfect places for an outdoor potted-bulb garden. From Boston to Santa Barbara, and Billings to Baton Rouge, gardeners are discovering the pizzazz that potted bulbs bring to outdoor living areas.

The advantages of container-grown bulbs are many. The potted-bulb garden, with its mobility, allows for great flexibility, providing greater freedom in culture and design than the immobile earth. No one garden, for instance, can accommodate the right conditions of soil, light, and water for every type of bulb. But by using pots, gardeners are able to extend their choices to a vast array of plants, each with a custom-made environment within the container. Potted bulbs are generally easy to care for, as the gardener controls the soil mix, fertilizer, drainage, and exposure. Pots of bulbs are less vulnerable to many pest, including rodents, slugs, and cutworms. Pots can be brought indoors to protect the plants from threatening weather.

Potted bulbs can extend the gardener's season of bloom. When frost has put an end to the growing season outdoors, potted bulbs can continue to bloom indoors for many weeks before they are stored for winter.

Planted with many kinds of bulbs, the container

garden is ever-changing; each week heralds the debut of another star. Ungainly post-bloom plants are easily tucked out of sight, allowed to complete their growth cycle so that they will bloom again next year. Bulbs complement a range of other types of plants, but they are particularly graceful with favorite annual flowers, which are also often displayed in containers. The addition of the bulbs expands the available options for bold combinations of color, texture, and form.

ALSTROEMERIA BLOSSOMS HOVER LIKE BUTTERFLIES OVER ANNUAL COMPANIONS.

A FRESH APPROACH

Today's gardeners may look back at the Victorian era with amusement, awe, or with a fresh eye. Many certainly find great delight in evoking the essence of the gardens of another time, while others appreciate the exotica for their unique qualities in the contemporary landscape, unincumbered by the influence of past fashions. Understanding the plants of the past adds immeasurably to the gardening pleasures of today.

Take what interests you from the outdoor potted-bulb garden. The first chapter reviews the nature of bulbs and presents an overview of the basic cultivation techniques. Cultivating true bulbs, rhizomes, tubers, and corms in pots is not difficult to learn; it simply requires creating a microcosm of the plant's native habitat. Selecting the right size pots, creating an appropriate soil mix, and proper planting go a long way towards producing a blooming pot of unusual flowers; and it allows for great freedom in your plant selection.

The second chapter introduces the marvelous possibilites for designing the bulb garden outdoors. Bulbs may be incorporated with annuals for spectacular results. Tropical bulbs add an exotic touch to outdoor living.

THE LOCKET-LIKE FLOWERS OF BLEEDING HEART, DICENTRA SPECTABILIS, **EXCITED VICTORIAN SENSIBILITIES.**

Finally, the plant portraits showcase hundreds of species and cultivars for this special garden. Individual traits, cultural idiosyncracies, and recommended uses are outlined. Historical and personal anecdotes put the plants in perspective. A comprehensive list of sources will aid you in obtaining any of these featured wonders of nature.

CHAPTER ONE

THE
BULBS
OF
SUMMER

A POT OF 'RED HONEY' ASIATIC LILIES, *above*, IS WORTH THE WAIT. TUBEROUS BEGONIAS AND COLEUS PERCH ATOP A PATIO WALL WITH 'FAUN' ASIATIC LILIES, *right*.

Summer and autumn flowering bulbs must be among the most overlooked of all the bulbs, especially for container culture. It's a diverse, fascinating, and adaptable group that rewards the gardener for scant effort. The only limitation to the myriad creative opportunities it affords is that of the gardener's time, ambition, and imagination.

When summer madness seemingly grips the entire country, retailers parade their most colorful blossoms. Geraniums, petunias, and impatiens—those non-stop sirens of summer—call to every winter-weary gardener from every nursery, corner market, and roadside stand. Their intoxicatingly brilliant flowers sometimes blind us to the fact that the season has just begun.

As enjoyable as many of the bedding plants may be, and as useful as they may be to provide continuity in our container gardens throughout the growing season, they hold few surprises.

A static planting—virtually the same from start to finish—doesn't excite me. There's no reason to rush out in the morning and see what's new. Anticipation keeps me going. A thing of beauty is not forever—in the garden, at least. It appears and fades all too soon, but it is a joy nonetheless. The moments that linger in my mind—planting a bulb, anticipating its appearance, and reveling in its prime—make gardening a never-ending pleasure. From start to finish, there is a daily adventure.

THE NATURE OF BULBS

Something of a miracle of evolution, bulbous plants have adapted in several ways to insure their survival against extremes in weather. As a result, bulbs and their kin, unlike any other kind of plant, can be stored for long periods, and then planted to flower in the coming season. They can be shipped great distances easily and without harm. Having evolved with the capacity to store quantities of food underground, they all have adapted leaves, swollen stems or roots. For convenience sake, most gardeners lump all bulbous plants together as "bulbs." This loose grouping includes true bulbs, corms, tubers, and rhizomes.

TRUE BULBS

A true bulb can be identified by an embryonic flower inside the bulb and a basal plate at the base of the leaves from which rises two or more fleshy scales (actually, modified underground leaves). During the fall, lilies suspend operations; the leaves and stems wither after the flowers have faded and enough food has been stored by the bulb for flowering next year. Stored at temperatures just above freezing, the bulb is in suspended animation, waiting for warmer temperatures to send out roots to pump in moisture and nutrients in preparation to bloom again. Examples of true bulbs include *Crinum, Eucomis, Galtonia, Haemanthus, Lilium,* and *Ornithogalum.*

Differentiating them from the rest of the bulbous plants, each true bulb contains an embryonic flower developed during the previous growing season. A cross-section reveals the flower nestled deep in the interior. Like a cake mix that promises perfection with only the addition of water, true bulbs guarantee success (soil and light must be added to the ingredients) just by following simple instructions.

All but the most careless treatment cannot stop the flower production of a true bulb. They need plenty of soil underneath their basal plates for root development, and the ones with elongated necks usually do best if at least the neck protrudes above the soil surface. Most summer bulbs lose their top growth when cold weather arrives and they have been lightly frosted. They are best stored in cool, airy conditions after the dead foliage has been trimmed off. Depending on time and space, the bulbs may be left in their pots or lifted and stored.

With corms, tubers, and rhizomes, however, good culture is necessary to promote flowering, for they do not contain the pre-formed flower of a true bulb; inside their fleshy rootstocks they are solid. The plants, which spring from buds or shoots, must be grown under the proper conditions to bring them to the stage where they will blossom. This may sound daunting, but it is not very difficult. Healthy, plump corms, tubers, and rhizomes need only very basic care—sun, soil, and water in the right amounts—to thrive. It is rare when crocus, dahlia, or a host of others, fail.

SNOWY BLOSSOMS OF 'WHITE MOUNTAIN' ORIENTAL LILIES CAP AN AUGUST DISPLAY.

**SWEETLY SCENTED ABYSSINIAN
GLADIOLUS**, ACIDANTHERA BICOLOR,
GROW FROM WELL-FED CORMS.

CORMS

Corms are modified stems, usually flattened in shape and usually covered in a tunic. Corms look like bulbs to most gardeners; corms of *Acidanthera* or *Crocosmia* might easily be mistaken for true bulbs.

A corm, however, initiates growth from the top, for it has no basal plate. A corm is a storage warehouse for food; cutting one in half (on purpose or with an errant spade in the garden) shows that it is solid.

The corms of *Crocus*, for example, shrivel as their resources are depleted, to be replaced by new corms, which grow on top of the old ones. Most corms will replace themselves completely over the course of the season, so they need feeding to accomplish the metamorphosis. Some corms go completely dormant, as true bulbs do, in response to heat and drought or cold. Some even require warmth during dormancy to fulfill their needs for next season's performance, just as others require cold.

TUBERS

A tuber may be either a swollen stem or an enlarged root connected to the stem or both The most recognizable of all tubers is the potato, but tubers vary in size and appearance. They are generally permanent structures without tunics, although a dark "skin" is common.

Growth emanates from one or more "eyes" found at the base of the older stem, and roots may grow from many points on the tuber. Tubers are planted horizontally or nearly so, with at least one growing eye attached to each division. They are often summer structures, native to climates of summer heat and rainfall. They need enough room in the pot for the roots to feed and increase in size, and respond to regular fertilization. Tubers, such as *Begonia*, *Colocasia*, *Dahlia*, and *Ipomoea* store food and water, and they dessicate during storage in dry environments.

RHIZOMES

Rhizomes are swollen, creeping stems. They may appear above ground or below the soil surface. Among the rhizomes are *Achimenes*, *Canna*, and *Curcuma*.

Roots are produced on the underside, and growth starts at shoots on the ends of the rhizome. Rhizomes must be planted just below soil surface to allow the roots to delve into the soil for nutrients. They also require regular fertilization, and the rhizomes are divided as the plants outgrow their quarters or to increase stock.

A DARK, NEGLECTED CORNER GLOWS WITH TUBEROUS BEGONIAS, LOBELIA, WISHBONE FLOWER, AND DUSTY MILLER.

PROBLEMATIC CLASSIFICATIONS

Some plants usually considered to be of a bulbous nature fall into a netherland, for they are neither bulb, corm, tuber, nor rhizome. They are certainly bulbous, as far as gardeners are concerned, but do not fit botanists' strict definitions. Botanists contend that *Alstroemeria* and *Anizoganthus*, for example, have nothing more than a thick rootstock; but, because of their culture, gardeners and nurseries care little about this distinction and often consider them bulbous plants. Drawing the line is a difficult proposition in the first place. Nature defies man's attempts to put each species into a neatly compartmentalized unit.

The kind of bulbous storage unit often varies from plant to plant even within a single genus, and it can be confusing.

HEAD START

Flushed with our winter success with narcissus, squills, and tulips, we plunge into spring planting with an unequalled enthusiasm. Most summer-flowering bulbs can be planted in containers outdoors as soon as the danger of frost has passed, although many benefit from a head start indoors. Gardeners in temperate areas of the continent start in March or April.

This is also the time to wake holdovers from their winter doldrums. Pots of *Agapanthus* (lily-of-the-Nile), *Crinum* (milk-and-wine-lily), and summer callas need a shot of fertilizer and a closer spot near the window.

Some bulbs are started in smaller containers inside and moved up to larger pots as they grow. This saves space when it is most needed. *Achimenes* (nut orchid), begonias, caladiums, summer callas; and cannas need this head start. A propagation mat—a rubber mat with heat cables inside—can be used to provide gentle bottom heat. The pots of tulips on the windowsill may revel in the cool air, but tropical tubers and rhizomes will fail without temperatures in the mid-seventies. (I should know: I rot some shivering caladiums every few years seemingly just to remind myself.)

There is little advantage to be gained by planting *Acidanthera* (Abyssinian gladiolus), *Dahlia*, *Galtonia* (summer hyacinth), or gladiolus indoors, except in short season climates. They will develop quickly outside when planted in May or June. A few bulbs, such as *Amaryllis belladonna*, have odd schedules and are potted later in the summer. Planting of fall-bloomers is also attended to later.

A SINGLE POT OF BRONZE-LEAVED OXALIS **ACCENTS PERENNIAL PLANTINGS,** *left.* **AN OLD WOODEN CHEST HOUSES ROBUST** AGAPANTHUS **AND ANNUALS,** *above.*

THE GREAT OUTDOORS

I direct my energy in summer to the garden outdoors, and even my house plants move out with me. More than a hundred pots of seasonal flowers swell the ranks on the patio, porch, and underneath pergolas of grapes and wisteria. Growing bulbs in pots extends my options, bringing the fragrance of Oriental lilies and Abyssinian gladiolus to a supper outdoors, while the exotic leaves of caladiums, colocasias, and cannas impart a bold tropical touch. Begonias and nut orchids brighten shady nooks, while sun-loving dahlias combine with annuals in overflowing pots.

The advent of autumn does not spell the end of surprises. Late bloomers, such as, *Colchicum* (meadow saffron), *Crocus speciosus* (autumn crocus), and *Nerine* (Guernsey lily) are even more cherished for their spring-like beauty that belies the inevitable end of the growing season. Even when frost threatens, a pot of them is easily wisked indoors.

SPLENDOR OF THE TROPICS—CALADIUM, COLEUS, AND ASPARAGUS FERN—THRIVE IN A SHADY, PROTECTED POSITION, *above left.* **GARDENERS VALUE 'CASA BLANCA' ORIENTAL LILIES,** *below left,* **FOR THEIR FRAGRANCE AND LATE BLOOM TIME.**

EXOTICA

Flowers that would not ordinarily thrive in my beds and borders, or that might be troubled by pests, are accommodated in pots. It may be impossible to control temperatures outdoors, but it is possible to prepare for them and use them to advantage.

Tropical bulbs, as a rule, grow poorly in cold soil. Garden soil heats up slowly in the spring, but the soil in pots, exposed to warm air around them, stays relatively warm, even at night. The forecast of a late arctic blast may dictate their move to shelter indoors, while the best that we can do for plants set directly in the ground is a blanket of newspapers.

Gardeners in temperate climates may long for the exotic bulbs, and there's no reason they shouldn't be able to enjoy them at home too, as long as they grow them in containers. Profusely blooming lily-of-the-Nile adds a cool note, while potted *Alstroemeria* (Peruvian lily) and *Sprekelia* (Aztec lily) invite a close-up inspection of their remarkable flowers.

Clay soil frustrates many bulb fanciers. A sticky mess when it rains, and adobe hard when it doesn't, clay is as inviting to most bulbs as a shot of herbicide. Their roots rot or can't penetrate through it. Most bulbs perish in clay, so the logical option is to enjoy them in pots of friable loam.

Even gardeners blessed with perfect loam, may have problems with voles, moles, squirrels, or slugs. It's open warfare in many gardens. The gardener is not always the winner. They tire of providing an open salad bar to varmits and give up on bulbs. Containers are not animal-proof but they minimize the damage, for burrowing and tunneling animals rarely bother a clay pot.

Freshly-planted bulbs are the most vulnerable to attack. I sometimes think that squirrels assume that I'm having a little Easter egg hunt just for their benefit. I plant the bulbs; they find them and dig them up. This is not my idea of holiday fun.

I store newly planted bulbs in the garage until they sprout, when squirrels find them less appealing. I also find that annuals planted immediately over the bulbs discourage them as well.

Slugs consider emerging bulbs among the tastiest of treats (right up there with beer) and it requires vigilance to protect lily tips from their voracious appetites. I sleep a lot better when my lilies are safely tucked in pots on the patio.

CONTAINERS

Choosing a container requires forethought when the bulbs are planted. How much water will it need, and how often, when the heat is on? How large should the pot be? The answers are: a good daily soaking, and bigger than I thought.

Soil insulates bulbs and roots from heat damage. A large container provides a little extra protection, allows for good root growth, and keeps watering to a manageable level. It takes only a few more minutes to water a hundred pots than it does to tend to five; the key is to make the task a daily habit.

A terra cotta pot is preferred by many, but clay heats up in the sun; a pot with an opening less than eight or ten inches across is virtually useless in warm areas. A bottom layer of styrofoam packing peanuts or straw helps to fill a deep pot, allows for better drainage, and prevents root rot from wet, stagnant soil.

Plastic containers are perfectly serviceable and evaporation is less. Aesthetic considerations, however, usually dictate that they be hidden in wicker baskets or ceramic pots.

Wooden planters of all sorts serve well for bulbs. Wooden containers make sense for large bulbous plants, such as *Agapanthus*, *Crinum*, or *Colocasia* (elephant's ears), especially those that are traditionally displayed outdoors in the summer but wintered indoors in their pots. Painted white or hunter green, wooden planters have long been a feature in conservatories and sun rooms. Wood has the additional benefit of being a good insulator, from both cold and heat.

The half whiskey barrel, long a uniquely American planter, has been increasingly sought by English gardeners. It affords the space to grow any number of plants, bulbous and otherwise, with a controlled soil mixture and good drainage. Their interest has made these durable barrels increasingly scarce and correspondingly more expensive.

An old-fashioned bushel basket, still relatively inexpensive, makes a perfect planter for the largest bulbs and tubers. Our grandmothers discovered its value long ago to grow geraniums. Wood is an excellent insulator; roots stay cool and a bushel basket drains well. Lilies especially appreciate this critical feature, for no other bulbs are as prone to rot in soggy soil. The only drawback to bushel baskets is their lack of permanence since the bottoms disintegrate after a

A TERRA COTTA POT OF OXALIS CRASSIPES **'ALBA' SHOULD BE CHECKED DAILY FOR DRYNESS.**

few years of service. I found this out when I picked one up by its wire handles only to have the contents plop through the bottom.

Other choices that must be evaluated individually for suitability include stone, cement, lead, man-made stone, cauldrons, and glazed pots. Sufficient size, depth, and drainage capability should be the prime considerations.

To make a good show, bulbs must be spaced fairly closely in a pot, but the needs and eventual size of the plants should be considered. Cannas, dahlias, and elephant's ears turn into enormous masses of leaves, while *Polianthes* (tuberose) and *Zephyranthes* (zephyr lily) produce comparatively sparse foliage, so it takes six or eight closely-spaced bulbs for a good show.

Plants that grow from corms, such as *Acidanthera*, *Gladiolus*, and *Tigridia* (Mexican shellflower), need to be spaced fairly closely to produce a lush, full effect, but they need enough room for each corm to develop fully and bloom. Fertilization and ample space are critical for these corms, as they flower only after the plant has grown strong enough.

A SUMMER PLACE

Bulbs grown outdoors must be positioned according to the extremes of the climate. Hot, baking afternoon sun invites disaster for most. Gardeners in cool regions, however, must endeavor to find microclimates against walls and on patios to trap all the heat and sunshine they can for the Mexican beauties like dahlias, tuberoses, and *Tigridia*.

It is surprising that many gardeners have never evaluated their outdoor living spaces to see just how much sun or shade is available. They might think that a particular plant they have just discovered at the nursery will look just dandy on their sunny terrace, only to discover that it stops blooming. They feed or water it to death without ever realizing the problem was the exposure.

Finding out what a bulb needs to survive is the first step. Experimenting is the second. The intensity of light varies across the continent, based on latitude and altitude. Some areas receive an abundance of sunshine while in others clouds predominate. Patterns of sun and shadow change throughout the season. Planning, guesswork, and discovering the micro-climates within your garden is the challenge.

Microclimates within the landscape will be very important for determining which plants will thrive in the garden. For instance, paved areas, brick and stone walls can provide areas where heat is trapped. Hedges, fences, and structures that block wind may be a boon in cool climates, whereas in warmer areas, gardeners may wish to cloak those walls with vines to cut down on the radiant heat. The quality of sunlight is a factor to consider when selecting a planting spot for any kind of plant. There are many degrees of shade. For example, some deciduous trees cast dappled shade, while evergreens cast dense, full shade. Arbors, pergolas, and gazebos can provide shade as well, the quality of which will depend on the construction and what vines, if any, are growing on them. Porches, terraces, and decks may make suitable homes for bulbs, depending upon their exposure to sunlight. In cool climates, southern and western exposures benefit sun- and heat-loving plants, while in areas where summers are particularly hot, these exposures may be too hot for the bulbs, or they may need diligent watering.

WOODEN CONTAINERS SUIT LILIES, *left*, **AND PINEAPPLE LILY**, EUCOMIS PUNCTATA, *right*.

SEASON'S END

No arbitrary timetable governs the final curtain for summer-flowering bulbs. The first frost dictates when the season is over outdoors, while shorter days signal indoor plants to close up shop. Water should be withheld from the stubborn ones to induce dormancy.

Tubs of plants that are to be wintered indoors should be wrestled inside when frost threatens. Some that have not finished their show, like dahlias, can be brought indoors for a few more weeks of enjoyment, but will cease flowering quickly in response to lower light levels.

While some bulbs, such as *Ipomoea batatas*, need special treatment, most bulbs can be dug up and stored. When the foliage has withered and the leaves are completely dead, the leaves of most bulbs can be cut off, and the bulbs dug out. Some plants, however, such as *Agapanthus*, may never totally lose their leaves, hanging on to them tenaciously after six months of drought. Most bulbs, rhizomes, tubers, and corms can be dug, dried (spread the bulbs out on newspaper for up to a week), and stored for the winter in paper or mesh bags, or in containers filled with sand or wood shavings kept barely moist to avoid desiccation. Where space permits, the whole pot can be brought indoors for the winter without disturbing the contents.

GARDENERS STAVE OFF WINTER BY COAXING A FEW MORE BLOSSOMS FROM TUBEROUS BEGONIAS INDOORS BEFORE THE TUBERS ARE DRIED AND STORED.

PATIO DAHLIAS BEAT THE FROST AND SHOW OFF FOR SEVERAL MORE WEEKS INSIDE
WITH SIGNET MARIGOLDS AND IVY-LEAVED GERANIUMS.

TO EVERYTHING THERE IS A SEASON

The bulb grower's year is a busy one with autumn and spring making the most demands on time. As summer fades to winter (and it does so differently and at a different pace in various areas), summer bulbs are put to bed just as winter and spring bloomers are prepared for active growth.

As in most gardening activities, even winterizing bulbs is an act of renewal. In temperate climates, even before the first frost, some may show signs of preparing for winter by dimished flowering or yellowing leaves. Frost blackens top growth of bulbs grown outdoors. The foliage and stems are trimmed back to within inches of the base of the bulb, corm, tuber, and rhizome. Discarded foliage goes into the compost to become future nourishment for other plants. What comes from the soil must be returned to it.

Each of us must determine the best place in our homes to over-winter dormant bulbs as well as those that stay evergreen but get little attention. I couldn't cope without my basement. Pots of evergreen lily-of-the-Nile and kangaroo paws camp in the laundry room at about 60° to 65° F., lit only by a small, south-facing window. Both are extremely drought tolerant and, although many of their leaves yellow and wither alarmingly, they receive no water for nearly five months.

Other pots of truly dormant bulbs line the basement stairway and are lodged in a former coal room under the stairs. It is a meter reader's nightmare to visit my

AFTER FROST BLACKENS CANNA LEAVES, TRIM AND STORE THE RHIZOMES FOR WINTER, *left.* "DAUGHTER" BULBS OF LILIES, above, MAY BE GENTLY SEPARATED FROM THE MOTHER IN AUTUMN.

basement, and I'm quite certain mine must wonder just how I manage to kill so many plants. The coal room is valuable since it stays at about 45° through most of the winter, and prevents tropicals such as cannas, begonias, and elephant ears from sprouting too early.

In regions where humidity is low, some bulbs may shrivel from lack of moisture. They should be checked periodically and watered sparingly if they are in pots, or sprinkled with water if they are stored in wood shavings in mesh or paper bags. Plastic bags invite rot. Being cautious about chemicals, I use only a dusting of sulphur when necessary to prevent mold and fungus, but that is a personal choice.

The rebirth of the summer bloomers begins after the new year begins. Light intensifies, and depending on their peculiar schedules (refer to individual plant portraits and "The Bulb Grower's Year" on page 124), the bulbs are brought back into active growth by resuming watering and, in some cases, by providing supplemental heat. Achimenes, cannas, caladiums, and begonias, for example, are often sprouted on propagatrion mats or with heat cables. Supplemental flourescent light is quite useful. I use ordinary shop lights, holding two ordinary cool light flourescent bulbs (and envy the lucky people with greenhouses).

Bulbs, corms, tubers, and rhizomes propagate themselves. It's the gardener's job to help them along. Bulbs make bulblets or "daughter bulbs", usually at their bases, which may be gently teased away from the mother in fall or spring. They can be potted individually. Cormels are miniature corms treated in the same manner.

Tubers are increased by cutting away a piece with an axillary bud, called the "eye," which will form a new plant. Dahlias, for example, may double in size in a single season, and may be cut into two or more sections as long as there's an eye on each piece of the former stalk, from which growth will start. Similarly, rhizomes are simply chopped into reasonably-sized pieces to increase stock.

A few plants, such as sweet potato vine, are best propagated by stem cuttings rooted in sand or perlite. Others, such as blackberry lily, grow best from seed and bloom the second year. Most bulbous plants may be grown from seed but some are agonizingly slow to flower. Hybrid plants will not come true from seed, but the process and surprise results intrigue many gardeners.

PERUVIAN DAFFODIL AND PAINT BRUSH COMPLETE THEIR SEASONAL CYCLES INDOORS IN TEMPERATE CLIMATES. THE FOLIAGE IS REMOVED AS IT WITHERS AND THE— BULBS MAY BE LEFT IN THEIR POTS OR REMOVED AND STORED UNTIL SPRING.

CHAPTER TWO

A SUMMER SHOW

TUBEROSES AND SUCCULENTS MAKE
PLEASING PARTNERS.

Many gardeners spend the entire year in a perpetual state of planning. Even as we plant the dahlias, we are thinking ahead to digging them up and storing them for winter. It's a good habit, but sometimes a preoccupation with chores outstrips our ability to enjoy what we've accomplished. Enjoying the dahlia blossoms somewhere in the middle ought to be penciled in on our calenders as well.

After a few seasons of growing bulbs in containers, the attention to detail need not be as accute. Mastering the basics is relatively simple. They either get potted early indoors or later outdoors, depending on how tender they are. The old friends, holdovers from previous years, are brought outdoors to do their magic again. With tender loving care, they grow, flower, fade, and are then stored for another year.

Bulbs kept in the same container should be top-dressed after the first or second year. Top-dressing is the removal and replacement of the top few inches of soil.

In the meantime, finding companion plants for summer bulbs and staging displays of the plants, indoors and out, makes growing them all the more interesting. Then there are those special moments, scarce as they seem in gardening, to sit down and enjoy the bounty of blooming bulbs around us.

A BOUNTY OF BULBS—ALSTROEMERIA, HYBRID ASIATIC LILIES, NERINE, AND OXALIS—GRACE A CALIFORNIA COURTYARD.

LOBELIA AND POLKADOT PLANT COMPLEMENT BEGONIAS AND THE IRIS-LIKE FOLIAGE OF BLACKBERRY LILY, BELAMCANDA CHINENSIS.

ANNUAL ADVENTURES

Container gardening ranks as one of the most popular and innovative aspects of gardening. Combining bulbs with annuals is a natural. Bulbs often become the centerpiece of a large pot or grouping of pots and annuals show them to best advantage.

Bulbs root in the lower level of soil with annuals on the top. Competion for nutrients requires supplemental fertilization for all of the occupants. A picture-perfect pairing of bulbs and annuals, seemingly cascading effortlessly from the containers, takes practice. While the plants need to be positioned tightly for a good show, ruthlessly jamming them in doesn't allow for growth.

Since they must share the same pot for the entire season, annual additions to bulb displays must also share the same cultural requirements. Sun and shade needs obviously segregate the plants, but moisture needs must be met as well. Globe amaranth (*Gomphrena globosa*) makes a perfect partner for pineapple lily because they both thrive in sun and do best when they are allowed to dry out a bit between waterings. Wishbone flower (*Torenia fournieri*) is a pretty complement for tuberous begonias, not only because the yellow throat of the little annual is the absolute best pairing with a yellow begonia, but because the two share the need for partial shade, high humidity, and constantly moist soil.

Some annuals make decidedly good mixers with bulbs. Few bulbs are noted for their extraordinary foliage (the exceptions, however, are quite exceptional) and are enhanced by plants that contrast them with different textures, shapes, and colors. Trailing plants, such as lobelia, ivy, vinca, sweet alyssum, nasturtiums, and lamiastrum, weave a planting together and spill out the sides, softening the hard edge of the pot rim.

Annuals with small but profuse flowers complement the stars of a grouping—the begonias, lilies, or liatris— without grabbing the spotlight. Signet marigolds, salvias, impatiens, and fibrous begonias play their parts well. They provide continuity to the grouping as well, and can tie together an area by repeating the same running threads of color.

Foliage annuals are invaluable to mix with bulbs. Though not as numerous as flowering annuals, those with outstanding leaves are diverse and useful. The feltlike, silver leaves of dusty miller provide the ideal lacy framework to showcase any pastel flower. The maroon, metallic leaves of Chinese basil (*Perilla frutescens*) do the same for orange or red flowers, such as those of some cannas, dahlias, or lilies. The varied leaves of coleus, that workhorse of the annual garden, break up

DARK SWEET-POTATO LEAVES TWINE THROUGH
FOLIAGE, *above*. SMALL ALLIUMS, *below*,
ARE BIG ON CHARM. CHINESE BASIL UNITES
TULBAGHIA AND ORIENTAL LILIES, *right*.

monotony. From spring green to deep red, or with the splashed markings of a Jackson Pollack canvas, coleus foliage never fails to provide interest.

Other noteworthy plants for combining with bulbs and other annuals include asparagus ferns, scented geraniums, copperleaf (*Acalypha wilkesiana*), polkadot plant (*Hypoestes phyllostachya*), spider plant, flowering maples, as well as any number of tropical houseplants.

Even the bulbous plants grown primarily for their own dramatic leaves often benefit from contrasting them with annuals. Cannas, caladiums, voodoo lily, and sweet potato vine look even bolder when a supporting cast of small-flowered or finer textured plants sprawl in their shadows or peep through their imposing foliage.

Sometimes a lovely effect is achieved by grouping pots containing one kind of plant with other "singles." Pots of begonias, for example, are especially pretty with those of sparkling blue *Browallia speciosa*. This works well when the same theme is repeated several times in one area.

Staging the plants—either on racks, shelves, or benches—is an art in itself. Most gardeners prefer a variety in pot sizes and heights, and use bricks or concrete blocks to raise some pots in a grouping. Matching pairs of potted bulbs and annuals flanking an entrance must be large enough to be appreciated. Rows of identical pots on a ledge or balcony impart a charm reminiscent of European villages. Pots are portable, and the gardener can rearrange throughout the season. I'm one of those fidgety ones who can't leave well enough alone. "Why didn't I think of that before?" I'll ask myself, as I grab a pot of yellow Peruvian daffodils and try it with the blue agapanthus.

It's a matter of scale, color, and texture, selecting partners for the bulbous plants, and then allowing them to work out the details. One of the pleasures of combining different plants together is visualizing what they will eventually look like. The plants sometimes have a different plan than the gardener, and it is these unexpected results that are so delightful.

A MOVEABLE FEAST

ALL EYES ARE ON 'GRAND CRU' ASIATIC LILIES, BROUGHT IN AS A LIVING BOUQUET WITH COLEUS, CHINESE BASIL, AND BRONZE-LEAVED PHILODENDRON.

Potted bulbs in their prime make living arrangements indoors. Some gardeners, including me, are reluctant to raid flower beds for bouquets. Bringing a pot of flowering bulbs indoors is only borrowing, and the house can be dressed up in just a few minutes. They can't stay in my dark living room for more than a few days, but that appeals to my recycling sensibilities.

Even the most devoted gardener can't spend as much time outdoors as they like. Moving pots inside brings the garden closer. A pot of caladiums on the work table or the office desk works wonders; studying the tracery of intricate veins certainly relieves boredom. Rain lilies on the breakfast table are as good companions as coffee and the morning paper. A grouping of potted begonias in the guest room says welcome almost as well as clean sheets, something of which my visitors shouldn't always take for granted.

Special occasions call for pulling out all the stops. It takes about ten minutes to create a centerpiece of lilies and begonias from the potted garden that will knock their socks off. I've been known to load up the truck for friends who were hosting special events; I wonder if my bulbs are going to more parties than I am.

Some bulbs grown outdoors can spend a week or two indoors with no ill effect. Most, eventually, will need to be returned to their places outside as soon as possible. Light is dramatically lower inside in most homes, and most plants accustomed to the intensity of

summer sun (even if they are in the shade) will signal their displeasure of the deprivation by dropping leaves or buds, yellowing foliage, or leaning towards the closest window. Put them back outside; the party's over.

A SINGLE SPHERE OF PAINT BRUSH, HAEMANTHUS MULTIFLORUS, **IS A BOUQUET IN ITSELF AND MATCHES FLOWERS OF GERANIUMS AND FIBROUS BEGONIAS.**

SUMMER
IN
THE CITY

A SUMMER HEARTH GLOWS WITH CALADIUM, FLOWERING TOBACCO, AND COLEUS, *above.* **A SKYLIGHT ILLUMINATES A POT OF** NERINE BOWDENII, *right.*

Apartment living need not condemn the gardener to a life with only spider plants and African violets for horticultural company. A sunroom or atrium often offers an ideal space for growing summer bulbs. Even a sunny window provides enough light to enjoy a vast array of bulbs.

Most bulbs, but not all, grown in the summer have high light requirements. Glass cuts the intensity of the sun's rays to an extent, but this should not affect their performance. Indoor temperatures cannot rise to Saharan heights, however, nor will a direct breeze from an air conditioner help matters. South or west exposures offer the most possibilities. Humidifiers enhance the performance of most tropical bulbs.

Likely candidates for culture under glass include begonias, *Achimenes*, and caladiums—all with lower light requirements. *Alstroemeria, Haemanthus*, lilies, *Oxalis, Nerine, Ornithogalum*, and pineapple lilies need very bright light but are relatively easy.

Window boxes and small balconies easily accommodate most of the smaller bulbous plants as long as they are kept well watered. Wind is a factor in high rise horticulture. It will tear leaves and topple top-heavy plants. Canna foliage catches the wind like sails, and I hesitate to advocate them for areas above busy sidewalks. Even a pot of tuberous begonias on the window ledge can catch a stiff gust and be hurled toward an unsuspecting pedestrian below.

Achimenes

NUT ORCHID

**THE JEWEL-TONED BLOSSOMS OF HYBRID
ACHIMENES BLOOM FROM MAY UNTIL FROST.**

While best known to gardeners for its velvety flowers, *Achimenes* has inspired a host of creative folk names. The tubers of *Achimenes*, for instance, which resemble tiny pine cones, or perhaps nuts, suggested the common name nut orchid.

In another instance, the Victorians discovered that, because the plants perform best where the environment most closely mimics their Central and South American homelands, mostly in shady, steamy rainforests, *Achimenes* sprouted best when placed near hot water pipes (due to the added heat and humidity). Recalling this innovation, the Victorians dubbed *Achimenes* the hot water plant, which has lead to the unfortunate assumption that the plants should be doused with hot water.

Most plants grown today are hybrids. The plants can grow to a foot or more, and by planting them rather thickly, the stems use each other for support and tumble gracefully out of the pot. The simple, serrated leaves form a dark green backdrop for the engaging flowers.

The tubers are best planted in mid-spring in a warm place—at least 60° F.—with a scant half inch of soil over the tubers. Well-drained soil, even moisture and regular fertilization suit these acid-loving plants, but beware of over-watering which can cause the flower buds to drop.

A close relative of *Gladiolus* (considered, in fact, by some experts, to be a member of that genus), *Acidanthera* distinguishes itself with beautiful and fragrant flowers. The plant was first introduced in 1896 from Ethiopia, then called Abyssinia, hence the common name.

The botanic name is derived from the Latin words *akis*, a point, and *anthera*, anther, referring to the sharply pointed anthers of the flowers.

The more vigorous variety of *A. bicolor*, var. *murielae* is favored over the species type. Its flowers display a more open, graceful spread and larger, triangular maroon patches on the pure white petals. Six to eight flowers, up to four inches across, are loosely spaced on arching stems over stiff, spiked foliage typical of the Iris family. These three-foot leaves earned *Acidanthera* the folk name of sword lily, which is sometimes used.

Acidanthera has staged an impressive garden comeback in the last few years as gardeners have rediscovered the sweet scent. The corms can be planted four inches deep at any time in the spring or early summer. A large pot, ten inches or more in diameter, and at least eight inches deep, can hold a dozen bulbs or more, with two inches between corms. Fertilized lightly and grown in a sunny spot, the flowers bloom for several weeks in August or September.

ACIDANTHERA

ABYSSINIAN GLADIOLUS

FRAGRANT ABYSSINIAN GLADIOLUS ARE A WELCOME ADDITION TO THE PATIO.

AGAPANTHUS

LILY-OF-THE-NILE

The common name lily-of-the-Nile evokes images of the fabled river and desert sands, and perhaps Cleopatra. The botanic name *Agapanthus* strengthens this association, translating as "love flower." Unfortunately, it throws the geography book off the barge, for these lovely blue-flowering bulbs originate in South Africa—on the other end of the continent.

Introduced to England early in the seventeenth century, these alluring flowers were among the first exotic African plants to be grown in Western gardens. Most plants grown today are classified as *A. praecox* subspecies *orientalis*, but may be listed as *A. africanus* or *A. umbellatus*.

Agapanthus, flowering as they do throughout most of the summer in sun, prefer afternoon shade in warm areas, but tolerate a wide variety of conditions. Large varieties are commonly grown in enormous wooden tubs (crowded roots are apt to break clay pots) that must be sheltered indoors in the winter. Smaller selected forms provide as much visual impact and are more manageable. 'Peter Pan', white 'Rancho Dwarf', and 'Queen Anne' are outstanding.

ELEGANT LILY-OF-THE-NILE FITS IN SURPRISINGLY WELL IN A COTTAGE GARDEN.

ALLIUM

ORNAMENTAL ONION

**EGYPTIAN ONION MAKES AN ENTERTAINING FOCUS OF
AN ECLECTIC MIX OF POTTED PLANTS.**

Anyone who has grown a convenient pot of chives (*Allium schoenoprasum*) to snip for salads and stews shouldn't hesitate to pot up ornamental onions. Some provide culinary extras, while others are quite pretty; most are both.

The lavender-pink blossoms of chives top a salad with panache, especially when combined with mandarin orange slices, and no bulb is easier to grow in a pot. Chives have long been a cook's staple; when Marco Polo journeyed into China in the thirteenth century, chives had been a part of the local cuisine for over three thousand years. It is likely that the Venetian traveler was responsible for introducing them to Europe.

Chives will thrive on a handy sunny ledge or bench just outside the kitchen. They can be sheared at will, with minimal damage to the plant. As the seasons turn, let the leaves sit in the frost, cut them back, and bring them indoors in the fall. They are exceedingly resilient plants, and an overlooked pot, left outdoors all winter (as I've done) will spring back to life the next year with no ill effect—although the treatment can be tough on a clay pot.

For sheer novelty and structural diversity, nothing beats the Egyptian onion (*A. capa* var. *aggregatum*). Almost more sculpture than vegetable, its hollow stems, a foot tall or more, are topped by clusters of bulblets. The weight of the maroon-skinned offspring eventually bend the stems down so they can root. Long in cultivation, the Egyptian onion is not known in the wild.

The chalk-white flowers of garlic chives (*A. tuberosum*) are a welcome addition late in the season. Thick umbels of flowers appear in August or September on eighteen-inch-tall stems. Native to Japan and India, garlic chives take well to pot culture, and can be used exactly like chives, making them a pretty accent in herb or vegetable gardens.

Many other ornamental onions—such as the late-blooming, lavender-pink *A. senescens*; its cultivar 'Glaucum', featuring twisted blue-green leaves; and *A. atropurpureum*, with deep ruby flowers make excellent potted plants. Winter them in a cold frame, unheated garage, or cool basement. Ordinary potting soil, regular moisture, and sunny conditions during the growing season are all that is required.

ALLIUM SENESCENS **SPORTS CHARMING BLOSSOMS ON LABOR DAY.**

Native to Peru, Chile, and Brazil, *Alstroemeria* goes by the folk names Peruvian lily and lily-of-the-Incas. Named by Linnaeus, for his friend Baron Claus Alstromer, the plants were brought into cultivation in Europe during the eighteenth century.

Large pots with a well-draining, organically-enriched soil mix suit the rhizomes. Plants can be left in their pots for several years, after which they can be carefully divided. They can be induced to go dormant by witholding water in fall or grown in a sunny window.

Most plants grown today are hybrids , especially of *A. ligtu* and *A. aurantiaca*, both from Chile. Hybrids bear six-petaled flowers in a range of vivid colors and pastels.

The parrot alstroemeria, *A. pulchella* from Brazil, bears blossoms in bands of green, white, and red. It grows well in southern gardens. In Texas it has been known as peanut lily ever since confused squirrels first dug up the peanut-shaped growths on the roots and buried them all about, inadvertently starting new colonies.

ALSTROEMERIA

PERUVIAN LILY

POTTED ALSTROEMERIA **HYBRIDS**, *left*, **BLOOM ALMOST CONTINOUSLY. CRINODONNA LILY 'SUMMER MAID'**, *right*, **TRUMPETS SWEET PERFUME.**

× AMARCRINUM

CRINODONNA LILY

A bigeneric experiment early in this century created the manmade genus × *Amarcrinum*, sometimes called × *Crinodonna*, the result of crossing *Amaryllis belladonna* with *Crinum moorei*. Carried out simultaneously but independently in 1920 by breeders in Italy and California (which explains the name dispute), the result is a plant with pink flowers like *A. belladonna* with evergreen leaves like *Crinum*.

The Victorians would have applauded this cloaking of the infamous naked lady with green underpinnings, finally making her respectable. A particularly fine variety of × *Amarcrinum* is called 'Summer Maid', which shows just how far the pendulum has swung. It remains to be seen which the public will prefer.

Clusters of the trumpet shaped flowers bloom atop leafless, purple-tinted stems in mid- to late summer. Most find their sweet fragrance, rich but not oppressive, particularly pleasing. Groups planted during the spring in deep pots may take a season to settle in before they bloom. × *Amarcrinum* are very easy to grow, and can be dried off and forgotten during the winter. I leave mine under the basement steps.

Other bigeneric hybrids include *Amarine* (the result of crossing *Amaryllis* with *Nerine*) and *Amarygia*, a product of *Amaryllis* and *Brunsvigia*.

AMARYLLIS

BELLADONNA LILY

The genus *Amaryllis* was once an enormous one. It is now comprised of a lone, albeit lovely, species, *A. belladonna*. The so-called amaryllis, a feature of yuletide celebrations, is now properly known as *Hippeastrum*.

Amaryllis was a popular woman's name in ancient Greece. Virgil named a shepherdess in his epics by the name, and for a time, all shepherdesses were called amaryllises. This is rarely heard today, perhaps because of the lisping nature of the word, as well as the lack of shepherdesses. I do recall that a pupil of the piano teacher Marion in "The Music Man" was named Amaryllis.

The belladonna lily, meaning beautiful lady of South Africa, has been cultivated since the eighteenth century.

A large, deep pot with sharply draining soil is suitable, and the bulbs should be planted with their necks just above soil level in late summer. Grow the leaves until they wither. Ignore the pot until midsummer when a good soaking will entice the appearance of "the naked ladies."

As many as ten fragrant flowers appear on each thirty-inch stalk. As the flowers fade, new leaves emerge, and watering is increased as the cycle begins again.

THREE-INCH FLOWERS TOP "NAKED" STEMS OF BELLADONNA LILY IN SUMMER.

ANIGOZANTHOS

KANGAROO PAW

The fuzzy, feltlike flowers of *Anigozanthos* exhibit a half plant, half animal look. It is small wonder that these Australian natives go by the name kangaroo paw. *A. viridis* goes one step further; its long, winking green "eyelashes" would fit right in with the Muppets.

Grassy leaves support sculptural stalks bearing clusters of the unique, long-lasting blossoms. Height varies by species and selection, and depends on light conditions, but ranges from two to five feet. *A. flavidus* sports yellow or apricot flowers. The stalks and flower bases of *A. manglesii*—the floral emblem of Western Australia—appear to be cloaked in crimson wool, and the green flowers contrast brilliantly.

Growing from rhizomatous rootstocks, frost-tender kangaroo paws thrive in well-drained, fertile, peaty soil in a sunny position. The evergreen plants should be kept moist and fed except in the fall and early winter when sunlight is weak. They are kept on the dry side during that rest period. Yearly repotting or top-dressing may be necessary.

FLORIFEROUS KANGAROO PAWS MINGLE WITH ANNUALS AND SUCCULENTS.

ARISAEMA

JACK-IN-THE-PULPIT

This eastern American woodland plant certainly cannot compete with tulips or daffodils for show, but the leaves and flowers are elegant and fascinating. The green- and chocolate-striped spathe (with Jack concealed within) rises on a stem above the foliage. Oblong leaflets are held in clusters of three, hence the designation *triphyllum*. The name of the genus, *Arisaema*, designates its kinship with *Arum*, the flowers of which also cloak themselves in hooded spathes.

The tuberous roots of *A. triphyllum*, called Indian turnip by early American settlers, can be planted in the fall, where they are protected in a cold frame or trench, or early spring and grown outdoors in a shady position. The soil should be enriched with compost or leafmold.

Jack-in-the-pulpit blooms outdoors on a shady patio in mid-spring. The leaves stay green throughout the summer, sometimes accompanied by red berries that follow the flowers.

BEGONIA

TUBEROUS BEGONIA

HOODED SPATHES OF JACK-IN-THE-PULPIT INVITE CLOSER INSPECTION, *left*. TUBEROUS BEGONIAS, *above*, GROW BEST IN BRIGHT LIGHT BUT SHIELDED FROM SCORCHING SUN.

egonias inhabit tropical and subtropical areas on all continents with the exception of Australia. With an estimated 1,000 natural species and countless horticultural varieties and hybrids, the plants display a remarkable diversity. The name *Begonia* is synonymous with elegant leaves and exotic flowers. It commemorates Michel Begon, an eighteenth-century governor of French Canada and an avid patron of botany.

The first *Begonia* species reached England in 1777, and a stream of newly discovered species flowed uninterrupted until the First World War. Among the greatest achievements of European and American breeders are the tuberous varieties, properly known as *Begonia tuberhybrida*.

Descended from wild species of South America, modern hybrids may be erect or pendulous, and exhibit a range of vibrant colors ranging from white through shades of yellow, salmon, orange, pink, and crimson. Flower forms vary so much that they are grouped by their types, including singles and doubles, and those that imitate the form of other flowers, such as the camellia-, carnation-, and rose-flowered types. The Bertinii group produces a profusion of small flowers.

Tuberous begonias grow from squat tubers with a slight depression in the top. Home gardeners customarily set the tubers under artificial lights in moist, fibrous soil in mid-spring because it takes twelve to fifteen weeks for the first flowers to bloom. The depressed part of the tuber remains above soil. Warm, humid conditions stimulate growth. The fleshy stems and large, pointed leaves are brittle and must be handled and staked carefully.

Begonias impart Victorian elegance to partially shaded porches and terraces. They make especially pretty pictures planted in large bowls or urns, where they associate exuberantly with asparagus fern, coleus, lobelia, and other old-fashioned annuals. In warm climates, it is essential to shade begonias during the hottest part of the day. Water and fertilizer are traditionally withheld in late summer, allowing the plants to yellow and wither. The tubers are then dug and stored at 50° F. in slightly damp wood shavings or moss.

THE 'NON-STOP' VARIETIES OF TUBEROUS BEGONIAS BLOOM VIGOROUSLY WITH LITTLE FUSS IN A WIDE RANGE OF COLORS .

BELAMCANDA

BLACKBERRY LILY

The flowers and fruit of *Belamcanda chinensis* invite close inspection, and potted plants offer two distinct visual treats. For several weeks in midsummer the freckled six-petaled flowers bloom in profusion. The two-inch-wide, yellow blossoms spotted with orange are all the more surprising, blooming as they do atop foliage that would seeming to promise iris flowers. *Belamcanda* is, in fact, closely allied to *Iris*. Though I cannot imagine any gardener putting it to any practical application in this country, its root is used as an antidote to cobra bites in India.

Introduced to Western gardens in 1823 from China, the plant boasts the delightful name blackberry lily for its fall surprise. The seed pods unfurl to reveal lustrous clusters of black seeds. Large pots planted with *Belamcanda*, marigolds, and salvias echo the change of seasons in a bright fashion. After frost, the stems of berries accent dried arrangements indoors. Winter pots in a cold frame, garage or basement, just above freezing, and keep them slightly damp.

BLACK BERRIES WILL LATER REPLACE THE BLOSSOMS OF BELAMCANDA CHINENSIS, *left.* THE MAN-MADE GENUS x PARDANCANDA, *above,* WAS CREATED BY CROSSING BELAMCANDA WITH PARDANTHOPSIS. THE MULTICOLORED FLOWERS ARE KNOWN AS CANDY LILIES.

CALADIUM

ANGEL WINGS

'CANDIDUM' OFFERS AN INTERESTING TEXTURAL CONTRAST TO SLEEK MARBLE, *above.* CALADIUMS GO COTTAGE-STYLE, *right,* OR INHABIT AN ANTIQUE FOOT BATH INDOORS, *far right.*

The rain forests of Brazil, Guyana, and Trinidad are home to *Caladium bicolor.* First discovered and introduced to Western horticulture in 1864, the exotic, intricately veined leaves made an instant impression on the Victorians who were enthralled by its tropical flavor. The scientific name is derived from a word from a native Brazilian tongue and means "unknown." I can only imagine a plant hunter asking his native guide the name of the plant, to which the guide answers "kelady."

The unknown species grows leaves up to thirty inches long under ideal conditions in its native habitat, and demonstrates a wide diversity of coloration and veining. It is the parent of a race of hybrids and selections—the fancy-leaved caladiums—called *C. hortulanum.* Bred extensively in this century in Florida, the heart-shaped leaves grow on narrow stalks and form plants from a foot to three feet tall. Small calla-like flowers sometimes develop, but it is the foliage that steals the show.

Started early in the year, the rhizomes needs warmth—a minimum temperature of 60° F. is a must—and moisture to sprout. Grow in bright, indirect light until night temperatures outdoors stay reliably in the upper 50s. Caladiums require protection from hot sun and wind. Pink, red, rose, cream, and white leaves are veined, splashed, streaked, and edged in seemingly infinite, mosaic combinations.

'Frieda Hemple' sports red leaves bordered

with green, and veined deeper red. The classic 'Candidum' displays dark green veins on a translucent white background. Paired with ivies, impatiens, or fuchsias, it fairly glows on an evening terrace.

CANNA

INDIAN SHOT

**ORNAMENTAL KALE CONTRASTS
END-OF-SEASON CANNAS.**

A terrace or patio brimming with summer flowers is a sight to behold. A bold stroke or two, cleverly positioned, will add drama and depth to the scene. Few plants embody the word "bold" as does *Canna*. The foliage alone qualifies as living sculpture, even without the vivid flowers. Why then, do so few cannas turn up on the terrace?

Like many good things, the Victorians grew cannas to excess. Carefully regimented rows, like faceless rows of chorus girls, still echo nineteenth-century sensibilities in municipal parks. When considered individually, however, cannas are flamboyant yet useful for pots and combinations.

More than fifty species of *Canna* grow in tropical and subtropical America and Asia. The name comes from the Greek *kanna*, meaning "reedlike," although it is not especially descriptive of the plant's long, broad leaves. The hard, black seeds of some species resemble shotgun pellets, from which the folk name Indian shot evolved.

Florida native *C. flaccida*, cultivated in gardens since late in the eighteenth century, is the principal parent of most modern cannas. Standard varieties can grow to four feet or more in a single season, and thrive in large pots with abundant moisture and sunshine. The cultivar 'Wyoming', in particular, is noted for its striking bronze

leaves and orange flowers. Another striking one is 'Black Knight' with maroon leaves and crimson flowers.

The German hybridizer Wilhelm Pfitzer raised valuable dwarf selections, including 'Primrose Yellow', 'Chinese Coral', 'Salmon Pink', and 'Scarlet Beauty'. Newer introductions offer promise and possibilities.

A VENERABLE WAGON TRANSPORTS 'BLACK KNIGHT' AND ANNUALS IN STYLE.

COLCHICUM

MEADOW SAFFRON

AS COLD WEATHER APPROACHES, THE DOUBLE-FLOWERED VARIETY 'WATERLILY' FINISHES ITS DISPLAY INSIDE, *above.* THE FLOWERS OF COLCHICUM AUTUMNALE SPRING FROM THE SOIL UNADORNED BY LEAVES, *below.*

The blooming of no flower is as eagerly anticipated in my autumn garden as *Colchicum.* They rise from the earth like glowing vases. *Colchicum* is all the more valuable for its springlike freshness and vitality coming so late in the season.

Named after Colchis, an ancient country bordering the Black Sea, the genus contains between fifty and sixty species mainly indigenous to Asia Minor, but some have been found in the wild as far west as Great Britain. Because the flowers—which more often than not are pink—energetically pop from the soil devoid of foliage, they are known in some quarters as naked boys.

Colchicum is often confused with autumn-flowering *Crocus,* as illustrated in one common name, meadow saffron. Beside botanical differences, *Colchicum* flowers are much larger and so is its springtime foliage: up to a foot long and half again as wide, its demise in the spring is exasperatingly long and unattractive.

All the more reason to grow colchicums in pots: in the spring one can deal with the foliage in seclusion. Potted in late summer, the corms quickly put on a bravura display. From six to twelve inches in height, the flowers of individual species, selected forms, and hybrids also vary in color and petal count.

Hybrids and selections from *C. autumnale,* *C. giganteum,* and *C. speciosum* comprise the bulk of meadow saffrons found in catalogues. Some, such as 'Violet Queen' and 'Autumn Queen', bear checkered markings on their petals.

The free-flowering hybrid 'The Giant' sends up foot-tall deep violet pink flowers with a white throat. Among the most sought after hybrids is 'Water Lily.' Its up to twenty lilac-pink petals open as wide as its namesake.

Slugs feast on colchicums, a fact I find disconcerting because they are poisonous to most animals, including humans. After they have bloomed, safe from slugs, in their pots, the bulbs can be overwintered in a cold frame or planted in the ground where they have to take their chances.

An old horticultural parlor trick was to place a brown corm on the windowsill and let it bloom "magically" without soil or water. Unsold bulbs in garden centers regularly perform this feat; I once saw an entire bushel basket turn into a living bouquet of pink blossoms. It's a mean trick, though, because any corm made to jump through such a hoop is thoroughly weakened. Without water and soil, its reserves are completely drained, and it will not often live to flower another season.

Colocasia

ELEPHANT EAR

THE SHIELD-SHAPED LEAVES OF ELEPHANT EARS, AIDED BY ABUNDANT
MOISTURE AND HIGH HUMIDITY, REACH FORTY INCHES IN LENGTH ON SIX-FOOT
PLANTS IN A LONG ISLAND GARDEN.

Growing up watching movies and television shows about Hawaii, I came to expect the inevitable *luau*. Drums beat, torches flared, women shimmied under grass skirts, and the revelers eventually feasted on roast pig and *poi*. I had no idea, years later, that the giant-leaved plant growing on my summer patio could bring me so tantalizingly close to a taste of *poi*, if not a *luau* itself.

Native to East Indies, *Colocasia antiquorum* variety *esculenta* is the potato of the tropical world. Its edible tubers are the source for the pastelike *poi*, which I find myself (on the advice of tourist friends) in no hurry to try. The cell tissue of colocasias contains sharp crystals of calcium oxalate which—if eaten raw—have the painful effect on the tongue and internal organs as tiny slivers of glass. Cooking the tubers for a very long time destroys the crystals.

The name *Colocasia* is derived from *kolkas*, which the plant is called in Arabia. It is known as taro, kalo, eddo, and dasheen in other lands. We call it elephant ears.

A pot of elephant ears dominates a serene pond, where it is often sunk to just below pot level. They set a grand backdrop for an exotic party, for a myriad of smaller companion plants, or for an afternoon of Polynesian daydreams.

EVEN IN A SEMI-ARID CLIMATE, AN UNDRAINED CROCK FILLED WITH WATER SUPPLIES THE ROOTS OF ELEPHANT EARS WITH ENOUGH MOIS- TURE TO ATTAIN IMPRESSIVE SIZE.

73

Of the hundred or so species of *Crinum*, only a few are cultivated. Growing from bulbs the size of a large bottleneck gourd, crinums produce thick foliage as long as four feet and stalks as much as four feet tall, carrying flowers of great beauty. *Crinum* comes from the Greek word for lily, *krinon*.

Two South African species are commonly grown. *C. bulbispermum* bears white flowers with a rose-colored stripe, and is sometimes called the milk-and-wine-lily (although the name is usually reserved for the Asian *C. latifolium*, whose similar flowers open for a solitary evening.) Scented *C. moorei* flowers in pale pink or white. A hybrid between the two, called *C. x powellii*, sends up flower spikes over two feet tall, carrying clusters of up to fifteen fragrant flowers.

The grand crinum of China, *C. asiaticum*, is sometimes found in conservatories. Its white spidery petals, three inches long but only a half inch wide, droop gracefully.

Crinum should be planted with the slender necks of the bulbs above soil level, in deep pots or tubs with organically rich soil. Except for moving them about, they are easy to care for in bright shade or filtered sun. Generous watering is in order in the spring and summer, while the bulbs should remain drier in winter.

CRINUM

MILK-AND-WINE-LILY

THE WHITE FORM OF CRINUM X POWELII **IS
ESPECIALLY LOVELY,** *above*. **MONTBRETIAS,** *below*,
DISPLAY STARRY ORANGE OR GOLD FLOWERS.

CROCOSMIA

COPPERTIP, MONTBRETIA

The spear-shaped leaves of *Crocosmia* indicate a kinship with *Iris*, but the flowers are distinctly different. Coppertip, *C. masonorum*, native to the south-eastern coast of South Africa, languished in obscurity until the variety 'Lucifer' ignited gardening passions. Above pleated leaves, the buds of the fiery flowers are arranged in pairs on the upper side of the stem, and open their vermilion petals in late summer. They thrive well in large containers, especially when watered well and given a place to bask in the morning sun.

Also growing from corms, the race of montbretias resulted from nineteenth-century crosses by nurseryman Victor Lemoine. The hybrids are called *C.* × *crocosmiiflora*, but in garden parlance they are known as montbretia. Their branching flowering stems zigzag from one alternately placed flower to another, and the funnel shaped blossoms open wide to reveal six rounded petals. Long-lasting montbretia flowers begin their display in midsummer.

Named varieties, blossom for a month or more in sunny shades of yellow ('Solfatare'), orange ('Emily McKenzie', and 'Lady Hamilton'), and red ('Vesuvius' and 'James Coey.')

'LUCIFER' SPARKS POTTED DAHLIAS, NICOTIANA, AND LAMIASTRUM.

CROCUS

AUTUMN-FLOWERING CROCUS

SAFE FROM A COLD SNAP, CROCUS SPECIOSUS OPENS IN A SUNNY WINDOW.

Autumn crocus rank among the easiest bulbs for almost instant gratification. Gardeners may wish to grow species in pots that are not suitable for their regions since some lovely species of autumn-flowering crocus are of questionable hardiness in very cold regions, and equally unhappy in very warm or wet ones.

C. speciosus, native to Turkey and Iran, is not only the easiest autumn-flowering crocus for indoors or out, it is among the loveliest. Blooming without foliage, the chalice-shaped flowers, up to eight inches tall, emerge gracefully from the soil. A bud is a beautiful thing in itself, and then opens to reveal a tracery of purple veins against the satiny petals. Golden orange stamens complete the picture. A succession of slender buds—usually three—emerge from each corm insuring several weeks of flowers. Companies offer selections with paler, darker, or larger flowers.

Wispy *C. kotschyanus* (better known in gardens as *C. zonatus*) from Lebanon grows reliably in pots. Less than half the size of those of *C. speciosus*, the pale flowers are tinted with lavender blue veining, with equally pastel straw yellow stamens. Container size is important. These delicate beauties can be lost in a hulking pot; a shallow, thin-rimmed container sets them off best.

C. sativus, saffron crocus, grows its foliage in the fall with the flowers. Native to Italy and east to Turkey, it blooms in pots if it is planted early enough, otherwise the flowers may be aborted. Its orange-red stigma, gathered for centuries for dyes and fine cuisine, can be plucked directly from the pot-grown lilac purple specimens. This is hardly a money-making venture, however, as it takes 4,000 dried stigmas—one from each blossom—to produce a single ounce of saffron.

The corms of autumn-flowering crocus should be planted as soon as they are available; often by September the corms show signs of sprouting. They can be packed in rather tightly, with just a half-inch between them, and covered with an inch of soil. I set the pots in the shade on the patio to root when the night temperatures are hitting below 50 at night. Squirrels may discover this cache of goodies, as they did mine, so some protective covering can be devised.

Shoots may show above the soil in as little as three weeks, and if freezing temperatures approach, the plants move to a cool porch or window, where growth accelerates. Aftercare is simple in a cold frame or cool greenhouse where they are ignored and kept slightly moist. Where conditions are suitable, and if the ground outside has not yet frozen, they can be quickly transplanted to the garden.

CURCUMA

HIDDEN LILY

Hidden lilies hold great promise for gardeners where hot, steamy summers prevail. They thrive where conditions provide constant moisture, heat, and humidity. Because they grow best in shady spots, or at least those protected from afternoon sun, they make ideal plants for the shaded terrace where sun-loving cannas won't work.

Tropical Asia, from India and Malaya to Australia, is home to more than sixty-five species of *Curcuma*. "Curcuma" is the Arabic word for the plants, which are closely allied to ginger lilies (*Hedychium* spp.). Valued primarily for spices, dyes, and starches extracted from their tuberous rhizomes, many are highly ornamental plants. The spice turmeric, an ingredient of curry powder, comes from *C. domestica*, for which in the tropics, especially Hawaii, it is widely cultivated. Turmeric is sometimes called Indian saffron, since it is used to dye rice and, occasionally, people. The bride and groom paint their arms with turmeric in traditional Indonesian weddings, while some Pacific island peoples decorate cheeks and torsos with the yellow dye.

The attractive, long, broad leaves—much like those of cannas but more closely bunched together—are often marked with a purple midrib. Plants grow from a foot and a half to three feet tall. The cone-shaped flower heads, five to eight inches long, consist of large bracts connected in such a way as to form pouches. Each pouch holds two or more small flowers—the hidden lilies.

C. elata and *C. latifolia* from India feature showy bracts of violet and red, respectively, with hidden yellow flowers. *C. australasica* from northern Australia is distinguished by rose-pink upper bracts. Those of *C. roscoeana* from Malaya are yellow-orange. *C. petiolata*, the queen lily, is native to India. It bears purple upper bracts with lower one of bright green, punctuated by yellow blossoms.

Plant the rhizomes in deep pots of organically rich, moisture-retentive soil. They are rested in their pots, usually losing their foliage, in the winter months indoors where temperatures drop no lower than 55° F., and are never allowed to completely dry out.

OUTSTANDING FOLIAGE AND ARCHITECTURAL FLOWERS OF A CURCUMA **HYBRID OFFER PROMISE FOR THIS RELATIVELY UNKNOWN GENUS.**

DAHLIA

DWARF DOUBLE DAHLIAS ADD DISTINCTION TO FINER TEXTURED SIGNET MARIGOLDS, IVY GERANIUM, AND ASPARAGUS FERN, *above,* **AND THEIR STIFF POSTURE IS SOMEWHAT SOFTENED. MIGNON TYPES,** *right,* **PERFORM TIRELESSLY WITH LOBELIA, NICOTIANA, AND DUSTY MILLER.**

The Aztecs cultivated species of their native *cocoxochtl*, perhaps for its blood red flowers, and certainly for medical uses. An Aztec herbal from 1582 shows a plant, its hollow stems resembling water pipes, indicating its use to treat urinary problems.

The first of the flowers to be grown outside Mexico and Central America reached Madrid in 1789. The curiosity spread among European horticulturalists, and Linnaeus named it *Dahlia*, in honor of his student Andreas Dahl. From the single red, pink, and purple flowers of wild species, a vast array of hybrids were produced. Even royalty got involved. Empress Josephine held the French monopoly on dahlias for a time, until one of the ladies of her court sweet-talked a gardener into procuring some for her. The display from the purloined tubers enraged Josephine, who banned dahlias from her garden, the lady from her court, and heaven knows what happened to the unfortunate gardener.

Enthusiasm prevailed, however, and devotees in Europe and America achieved an impressive color range of flowers, from white and yellow, to orange, red, violet, and pink, as well as bicolors. Flower shapes were manipulated as well, forming stars, pompons, doubles, and those that imitate other flowers, such as peonies, cactus.

The introduction of 'Coltness Gem' in 1922 changed everything. Here was a dwarf plant that bloomed throughout the summer. So-called patio dahlias were born. Suitable for the front of borders, for window boxes, or containers, smaller dahlias bloom profusely in vibrant shades and many forms. Mignon types, less than eighteen inches tall, produce single flowers. Collarette types feature one or more series of rings of shorter petals, usually of a contrasting color, on top of the main ring of ray petals surrounding the center disc. Dwarf varieties also exist in the peony-flowered, double formal and informal, and cactus-flowered groups.

Sun- and moisture-loving dahlias grow quickly from tubers planted in pots several weeks before the threat of frost has passed outdoors. Regular feeding promotes growth, but the amount of nitrogen should be curtailed for it encourages leaf growth at the expense of the flowers.

After the first light frost, which should not harm the tubers, the plants are cut back to just several inches of stalk with the tubers attached, and stored in moistened sand or shavings. When planting them the next year, a piece of the old stalk must remain attached to each division, for unlike potatoes, sprouting "eyes" do not occur scattered over the surface of the tubers.

DICENTRA

BLEEDING HEART

Strung on delicately arching stems, the dangling, deep pink hearts of *Dicentra spectabilis* looked like heirlooms even when they were introduced to gardens early in the nineteenth century. Gardeners of the day, perhaps more sentimental than we, doted on the new treasures, which they also called lyre flower and lady's locket.

These spring beauties of the border, become disheveled messes later when the foliage withers. *D. spectabilis* does not do a disappearing act for everyone; cool summers suit this native of Japan and Siberia.

Potted specimens solve the dilemma. The tuberous perennial can be displayed in their prime, and hidden afterwords. They are especially pretty housed temporarily in large urns reminiscent of their Victorian heyday, and replaced with caladiums as they fade.

The ever-blooming bleeding heart, *D. eximia*, makes a handsome container plant for the entire season. (I'd take it over a marigold any day.) It needs almost no maintenance to appear crisp and neat, as the flowers drop inobtrusively.

DICENTRA EXIMIA, *above*, **FLOWERS IN A CLAY CLOCHE.** DIETES IRIDIODES, *right*, **IS A WINTER TREAT IN A WEST COAST GARDEN.**

DIETES

WILD IRIS

Counterparts of northern *Iris*, *Dietes* are found chiefly in South Africa. Most gardeners think the flowers look like exotic, wild iris and they are right.

Perhaps the best-known species is *Dietes iridiodes* (*Moraea iridiodes*) native to the eastern Cape Province northward. Above dark, leathery evergreen leaves rise slender stems up to two feet tall. They are topped by graceful white flowers, two inches across, bearing small orange patches. One form flowers in late summer and fall while another (with broader leaves) is a late winter and spring bloomer, but both will produce flowers sporadically throughout the year.

Flowering in spring and summer, *D. grandiflora* is similar except for its four-foot height and broader, four-inch-wide leaves. The flowers of two-foot-tall *D. bicolor* are cream blotched with brown at the petal base and appear in spring and into summer. Both originate in the same area as *D. iridiodes*.

Gardeners in mild climates have been cultivating the plants for many years, but these tender beauties are rarely seen elsewhere. They may be successfully grown in pots if they are sheltered from frost indoors in winter. Abundant moisture is necessary while they are flowering but they are drought tolerant.

THE DELICATE PETALS OF ERYTHRONIUM **'PAGODA' UNFURL AT TULIP TIME.**

ERYTHRONIUM

TROUT LILY

Gardeners have been so bewitched by the wiles of *Erythronium*, that wherever they thrive—mainly in temperate North America and Europe—the flowers have collected poetic folk names. With their graceful, nodding blossoms hovering over handsome leaves, they make quite a picture in spring. The plants have been variously dubbed the trout lily and fawn lily, for the marbled foliage; adder's tongue, for the shape of the leaves; dog's tooth violet, for the shape of the corms (not the flower petals, as one might expect); and avalanche lily, for their mountain habitat. The scientific name is a mouthful, and is derived from the Greek *erythros*, meaning red. The name is as ancient as any botanical term; originally it was used for an altogether different plant.

Growing from fleshy corms and native to damp woodlands and mountain meadows, species of *Erythronium* grow well when planted in pots filled with moist, humus-enriched soil. Planting fresh corms upon arrival is the best approach for success.

E. americanum, from eastern North America, bears solitary yellow flowers on stems four to six inches high. The beautifully mottled leaves of European *E. dens-canis* set off the strongly reflexed petals in variable shades of pink and rose purple. The authentic dog's tooth violet resembles a cyclamen in its airy grace, and has been cultivated since the sixteenth century.

There is no ugly duckling in this family. 'Pagoda', a selection of *E. tuolumnense* from woods of the Sierra Nevada Mountains, may be my favorite swan. Its pendant, sulphur-yellow flowers on foot-tall stems exhibit an Oriental elegance that belie the plant's vigor. Half as tall, *E. revolutum* 'White Beauty' (actually cream yellow with golden patches on the interior) is a comely selection of the Pacific coastal species, while 'Rose Beauty', at more than a foot, demonstrates the species' variability in size and color.

EUCOMIS

PINEAPPLE LILY

Who could resist growing pineapple lily on the terrace, if only to enjoy the puzzled faces of visitors who stop, stare, and ask, "What is that?" There is a joy in cultivating horticultural oddities, especially easily-grown ones like *Eucomis*. The plants are extraordinary, really, with the tuft of foliage at the top of each flowering stem—like the topknot of a pineapple fruit—adding whimsy to its beauty. The name *Eucomis* comes from the Greek *eukomes*, meaning beautiful headed, and I have no trouble picturing Venus wearing a similar seaweed green turban on temple-cleaning days.

Eucomis is, as might be expected, native to South Africa, where unusual plants are the norm rather than the exception. Suitable for patio or terrace, greenhouses, or window garden, the cylindrical flowering stalks rise from one to three feet in height above spreading rosettes of bright green leaves. The stalks of *E. comosa* are studded with small, six-petaled blossoms in shades of white or pink. The individual flowers of *E. bicolor* are tinted pale green and the petals are carefully outlined with a thin purple stripe.

The broad leaves of *E. autumnalis* (formerly known as *E. undulata*) are unmistakable for their wavy margins, topped by stems of pale green or white flowers with the characteristic crown of green leaves. New hybrids promise a greater color range, bigger blossoms, and larger flower heads.

Pineapple lilies should be planted with the neck of the bulb just at the soil surface, in well-drained soil, shaded from the hottest of the afternoon sun, and watered well during the summer. The bulbs rest in fall and winter and can be lifted and stored like dahlias.

EUCOMIS AUTUMNALES **FLOWER BENEATH A TUFT OF LEAVES, A LOOK THAT INSPIRED THE NAME PINEAPPLE LILY.**

GALTONIA

SUMMER HYACINTH

Although *Galtonia* bears a superficial resemblance to spring-flowering *Hyacinthus*, in differs greatly in its cultural requirements, origin, flowering time, and most importantly, size. Growing to up to four feet in height, the upright flowering stalks of the so-called summer hyacinth bear pendant white flowers for many weeks in late summer and early autumn.

The name *Galtonia* honors the British scientist Sir Francis Galton (1822-1911), who traveled widely in South Africa, home of the bulbs, and was an early advocate of using fingerprints as a means of identification. *G. candicans*, the only commonly grown species, is native to the Cape Province and has been cultivated since the mid nineteenth century.

It is sometimes called cape hyacinth, but despite the association with the heavily perfumed spring bloomer, and claims to the contrary, my nose has trouble detecting any discernible scent. Nevertheless, each stalk bears thirty or more, two-inch, pure white flowers.

GLADIOLUS

SPEAR LILY

Of the more than 200 species of *Gladiolus* native to Africa and Europe, few are cultivated, but the progeny of a selected handful became the flashy gladiolus hybrids, known the world over. They evolved from intense breeding begun early in the nineteenth century in Europe.

The cormous plants were known to the Romans, who dubbed them sword or spear lily, from the Latin *gladius*. A fixture in gardens and greenhouses for more than a century, hybrids are divided into six main categories. Those most amenable to summer pot culture are the nanus or dwarf group, called *G. × colvilli*, derived from two South African species, *G. cardinalis* and *G. tristis*. (Oddly enough, *G. tristis*, sometimes called the evening-scented gladiolus, is often grown indoors in winter for its sweet blossoms, but its offspring lack its scent. See *The Indoor*

Potted Bulb for more information on growing *G. tristis*.)

These dwarf hybrids of the *G. × colvilli* group, named for the Chelsea nurseryman who first produced the cross in 1823, grow to eighteen inches or less in height. They thrive in large pots in a sunny position, and benefit from protection from searing afternoon sun.

Among the many hybrids available, often labeled as miniature, nanus, or baby gladiolus in catalogues, the very old hybrid 'The Bride' is still a favorite for its pristine white blossoms. 'Impressive' lives up to its name, displaying coral flowers marked with rose markings.

One species that is frequently grown in the garden, *G. byzantinus*, can also be successfully grown in a pot. Native to Spain, Italy, and North Africa, its wine red flowers are borne on arching fifteen-inch stems.

THE COOL, STATELY BEARING OF SUMMER HYACINTH, *above*, ASSURES THEM A PROMINENT POSITION; A LARGE POT IS NEEDED FOR THE BIGGER-THAN-TULIP-SIZE BULBS. 'IMPRESSIVE' GLADIOLUS, *below*, THRIVE IN FERTILE, WELL-DRAINED SOIL.

HAEMANTHUS

PAINT BRUSH

While exotic plants are the rule rather than the exception in South Africa, the delightful *Haemanthus* invite comparison with some of the more familiar "puff ball" alliums. Even so, they create quite a stir when they bloom on my patio. Many of the fifty species bloom in shades of red, signified by the name *Haemanthus*, which is derived from the Greek *haema*, blood, and *anthos*, flower. (*Haemanthus* has been split in two—half are now labeled *Scadoxus*.

Variously called blood flower, torch lily, Catherine wheel, and shaving brush, *Haemanthus* is best suited by the name paint brush, fitting for their fancied resemblance to a housepainter's brush, albeit one that has seen better days.

H. katherinae (now *Scadoxus multiflorus* subspecies *katherinae*) is found in the Natal and Transvaal Provinces of South Africa. Bulbs produce four or five veined leaves, up to eighteen inches long, and spherical salmon-orange flower heads eight inches across on stems up to two feet tall. The flowers bloom in mid- to late summer.

The rounded, leathery leaves of the evergreen *H. albiflos* remind me of those of *Phalaenopsis* orchids, so the dense umbels of white flowers with orange stamens come as a surprise. This native of the eastern Cape and Transvaal Province encases its flowers in a white or pale green bract. Though they appear on thick stems that rarely stand upright, the effect is rather more graceful than might be imagined. Attractive red berries replace the flowers for a long season of interest.

H. multiflorus (now, unfortunately, *Scadoxus multiflorus* subspecies *multiflorus*) often blooms in midsummer without its leaves, sending up six-inch coral-red spheres of many tiny flowers. Its spring-green leaves, six inches long, emerge as the flowers fade.

Plant in well-draining, gritty soil, with added organic matter and top-dress annually in the spring. Protect them from strong afternoon sun, and water normally until fall, when the leaves wither. Except for *H. albiflos* they require no supplemental moisture until they awaken again the following spring.

HAEMANTHUS **PREFER CROWDED QUARTERS AND CAN REMAIN IN THE SAME POT FOR AS LONG AS FIVE YEARS.**

HEDYCHIUM

GINGER LILY

Gardeners in the deep South have long valued ginger lilies for their bold foliage, dramatic flower spikes, and ease of culture. Wherever warm, humid summers prevail, however, these relatives of *Curcuma* may be grown successfully. Native to tropical Asia, only a handful of the fifty species of the ginger family are widely available.

Comparisons to *Curcuma* and *Canna* are inevitable. Up to six feet in stature, with long, wide foliage, ginger lilies produce attractive, often scented, flowers in dense, showy heads. The long, protruding stamens of the flowers add an exotic grace.

The name *Hedychium* is derived from the Greek *hedys*, sweet, and *chion*, snow, in reference to the fragrant, white blossoms of some species, notably *H. coronarium* from India, Burma, and Ceylon. Known as the white ginger lily or garland flower, it sports a foot-long spike of sweetly scented flowers four inches across above four- to six-foot clumps of green leaves.

Equally tall and impressive, the kahili ginger lily, *H. gardneranum* from the Himalayas, bears a loose raceme of flowers up to a foot and a half long. The honey-yellow blossoms showcase a prominent red stamen. With more compact spikes of highly fragrant, pale yellow flowers, *H. flavescens* from India also attains five or six feet in height. Excellent hybrid ginger lilies display white, cream, yellow, or pale pink flowers often with pink or orange stamens.

Large tubs or pots are suitable for the tuberous rootstocks of ginger lilies, which may be positioned in sunny or part shady locations. Fed and watered regularly, these tropical beauties make a grand statement. Rest the plants in the fall as they finish flowering by reducing watering, and move them to a winter position indoors with a minimum temperature above 50° F. Resist cutting back old foliage until new, spring growth is well underway. If no room is available for the plants, dig and store the tubers like those of cannas and repot in the spring.

HEMEROCALLIS

DAYLILY

Few gardeners need an introduction to the stalwart daylily of the perennial border. The appropriate name stems from the Greek words *hemera*, day, and *kallos*, beauty, since individual blossoms last but a single day.

Scant attention has been focused in the past on growing daylilies in containers. The introduction of smaller hybrids that bloom profusely throughout most of the summer—a triumph of breeder's skills—places them among the best plants for large terrace containers. Golden yellow 'Stella de Oro' lead the revolution as one of the first long-blooming hybrids (even if its name is something of a linguistic corruption), and others will not doubt rival its popularity. The old-fashioned kinds, such as tawny daylily, *H. fulva*, should not be neglected, since their arching foliage is a season-long asset combined with annuals in containers.

Container-grown daylilies can be "healed-in" at the end of the season in the garden, or the tubs may weather cold winters with little additional protection.

BROAD LEAVES SET OFF EXOTIC HEDYCHIUM GARDNERANUM **FLOWERS**, *above.* HEMEROCALLIS FULVA **BLOOMS WITH LIATRIS**, *below.*

HYMENOCALLIS

PERUVIAN DAFFODIL

FRAGRANCE IS AN ADDED BONUS WHEN
LOVELY HYMENOCALLIS NARCISSIFLORA OPENS,
above. FOLIAGE IS THE FOCAL POINT WHEN
'BLACKIE' SWEET POTATO TUMBLES FROM A
POT, *right,* ALSO FEATURING LOTUS VINE,
TRI-COLOR SAGE, DUSTY MILLER, MEXICAN
FIRE BUSH, AND VARIEGATED DRACAENA.

I had no idea when I first grew Peruvian daffodil many years ago that it would become an indispensable feature of my summer terrace. I look forward to the unfolding of its buds as eagerly as I do lilies or roses.

Formerly classified as *Ismene* (the name under which I first grew it and still in use in many catalogues) Peruvian daffodil now goes under the rather clumsy scientific name *Hymenocallis*, from the Greek *hymen*, membrane, and *kallos*, beauty. It refers to the membrane that unites the stamens and forms the central daffodil-like cup. Six petals flare outward and back, creating a flower of drama and breathtaking beauty.

H. narcissiflora grows in high, rocky fields of Peru, although it is not hardy. Flowering spikes up to two feet tall rise above straplike leaves resembling those of amaryllis. Two to five deliciously fragrant blossoms appear in mid summer. The hybrid 'Sulphur Queen' displays pale yellow flowers with a green cast. Four hours of direct sun and liberal fertilization allow the bulbs to restore energy for blooming in subsequent years. The bulbs may be stored in their pots during the winter and kept dry after they lose their leaves.

IPOMOEA

SWEET-POTATO VINE

Some of my fondest childhood memories are of "kitchen sink gardening." I sprouted a garden of frilly carrot tops and lined up toothpick-impaled avocado pits suspended in the necks of water-filled jars on the windowsill. My most successful venture was with the sweet potato vine, similarly grown, that quickly overwhelmed its spot in the kitchen and ended up in my bedroom, twining across my dresser and looped around curtain rods.

I haven't thought much about my boyhood bedroom jungle vine for years, except perhaps at Thanksgiving dinners where I've finally come to enjoy the taste of sweet potatoes. Imagine my surprise when one of the hot plants of recent years turns out to be nothing more than a "designer" form of *Ipomoea batatas*.

What was that vine with the striking maroon leaves I kept seeing at Wave Hill, Chanticleer Garden, and the Scott Arboretum? I've learned it was the variety 'Blackie' and my friend Jane from East Hampton gave me a start to stuff in my luggage. It is as easy to grow as any other sweet potato vine (some things you never forget)

and makes a wonderful addition to patio pots. It is especially pretty with silver leaves and purple or red flowers. While 'Blackie' may be especially valued for its dark leaves, ordinary green-leaved sweet potato vines should be considered for a cascade effect in mixed containers as well.

Belonging to the morning glory family, sweet potato is botanically distinct from the ordinary white potato (*Solanum tuberosum*) and the yam (*Dioscorea alata*). The tuber is native to tropical America and is widely distributed around the world as a staple food. The tuber is easy to sprout in water or ordinary potting soil and grows rampantly in warm weather with abundant water. Bring pots indoors when frost threatens, trim back the vines, and continue to enjoy them.

Cuttings root easily; but do not cut the tuber in pieces to increase your stock as you would with an ordinary potato. Sweet potato tubers may also be stored for the winter after "curing" them for several days (perhaps near a hot furnace) to dehydrate them somewhat since uncured tubers will not keep through the winter.

LIATRIS

GAYFEATHER

Gayfeather revels in the summer sun and heat, sending rigid stems skyward in July. An atypical member of the daisy clan, *Liatris* further distinguishes itself by uniquely opening its flowers from the top of its stem downward, resulting in a long display. The tiny, fluffy flowers stud the upper half of the erect stalks, while thin, grassy leaves cloak the lower portion.

The corms of the North American plains natives should be planted just below the surface of the soil; deeper planting often results in poor flowering. *L. spicata* and *L. punctata* grow well in pots, and flowering spikes reach as much as two feet in height. While the plants normally flower in shades of lavender purple, white flowering forms such as outstanding 'Floristan White' possess an understated beauty.

A SOON-TO-BE SWALLOWTAIL BUTTERFLY IS NOT BEGRUDGED A FEW LEAVES OF LIATRIS SPICATA GROWING IN A CARPENTER'S BOX WITH MARIGOLDS AND SALVIA.

LILIUM

LILY

Lilies were formerly considered fussy bulbs, but that reputation has been erased by the legions of dependable beauties, many of them developed in the last half of the century by dedicated American breeders. True lilies, native to the northern hemisphere, are distinguished from daylilies (*Hemerocallis*) in that they grow from bulbs, produce straight stems with short leaves, and the blossoms last for more than one day. Some possess a powerful, hypnotic fragrance.

While some species of *Lilium* make dramatic pot specimens, such as Chinese coral lily, *L. pumilum*, Madonna lily, *L. candidum*, and the ever-popular Easter lily, *L. longiflorum*, most container-grown lilies fall into three hybrid groups.

Asiatic hybrids glow in pure hues, from deep red, shocking orange, and brilliant yellow to frosty sherbet shades of peach, pink, and cream. Bi-colored and spotted blossoms abound, and the aptly named brushmarks sport contrasting strokes on each petal. Asiatic hybrid flowers may be up-facing, out-facing, or pendant. These early-summer blooming hybrids range in height from a mere foot to five feet in height. While it may seem desirable to grow the dwarf varieties in pots, there is nothing like a pot of the towering stems of statuesque 'Yellow Blaze', brilliant vermilion 'Viva', or pale apricot 'Chinook' to make an unforgettable statement.

Many of the trumpet lilies, sometimes called Aurelian lilies, rise to equally impressive heights, although smaller hybrids have been bred for container growing. Trumpet lilies waft their sweet perfume in July and August, and set a magic mood for an outdoor evening supper. Colors range from white—often with the outside of the petals marked chocolate or green—to yellow, pink, and golden orange.

Oriental lilies, sometimes called rubrum lilies, bear enormous flowers late in the season that compete with orchids in their beauty and fragrance. Pink, crimson, and white colors predominate; most petals bear raised, darker-colored spots. The height of Orientals varies greatly. Diminutive raspberry red 'Stargazer', pure pink 'Gigi', 'White Mountain', and seashell pink 'Nancy' stay under two feet and require no staking.

Lilies require organically-rich, exceedingly well-drained soil, and suffer when the bulbs get too warm; potted lilies should be protected from the hot afternoon sun. I grow annuals to shade their "feet" and I've found that bushel baskets make the very best containers.

THE BLOSSOMS OF 'GIGI' ALMOST INVITE A SONG, *above left*. POTS IN A SHADED COURTYARD EXPLODE WITH FRAGRANT ORIENTAL HYBRIDS, *below left*. 'WHITE MOUNTAIN' GAZES UPWARDS, *above*.

LYCORIS

MAGIC LILY

There is no disputing the allure of these flowers. It is all the more fitting that they bear the name of Lycoris, a Roman actress (reputedly of great beauty, although no one mentions her talent) who was a mistress of Marc Antony. This was in the days before the tribune sailed off to Egypt into the arms of Cleopatra and impending doom.

Natives of China and Japan, no species of *Lycoris* is recorded to have entered western gardens until the mid-eighteen century, so it is doubtful any of the participants in the spicy ancient affairs ever beheld the flowers.

Lycoris grow and bloom on an unusual schedule. Planted in midsummer with the tips of the bulbs just at the soil surface and watered thoroughly once, the flower stalks—devoid of leaves—rise from the pot after a month or more. Small wonder that the most common species, *L. squamigera* from Japan, has been dubbed magic or resurrection lily. Clusters of the four-inch long trumpet-shaped blossoms on two foot stems and brighten the late summer scene with their rosy lilac hue. Thin leaves up to a foot long follow after the flowers have faded. The foliage should be watered, fed, and protected from early frosts; pots are rested during the winter after the foliage has died down.

Other species require similar treatment. *L. radiata* from Japan and China bears the common name spider lily for its dense heads, carried on slightly shorter stalks, of scarlet or deep pink flowers; each blossoms projects elegant long anthers. The golden spider lily, *L. aurea*, indigenous to China, Taiwan, and Burma, turns heads with its golden yellow flowers carried on stems growing to two feet in height.

It is heartening that container grown bulbs actually flower better than they do in the garden since *Lycoris* rarely survives winters. Some gardeners plunge pots into the soil to put a late zing into their borders.

LYCORIS SQUAMIGERA **RISES FROM ITS POT,** *right*, **SURPRISING THE GARDENER.**

NEOMARICA

APOSTLE PLANT, TWELVE APOSTLES

Who am I to dispute the belief that only with a fan of a dozen leaves will plants of Neomarica produce flowers? I make it a point never to count the leaves of an apostle plant, also known as the twelve apostles. Native to tropical America, the fifteen species of *Neomarica* of the iris family look every inch like an exotic iris. Previously known as *Marica*, named for the nymph of Greek mythology, the "neo" was added when botanists cleaned house and discovered the synonym for the related genus *Cipura* was also *Marica*.

Brazilian *N. longifolia*, the best-known species, grows two feet tall and displays canary-yellow blossoms, two inches wide, cross-barred with brown markings in the center.

Few gardeners take advantage of their ability to stand up to sweltering heat. Pot the rhizomes in soil enriched with organic matter and water regularly. They can be wintered in a bright spot where temperatures stay above 55° F. Watering is reduced somewhat during this resting period, which is also the best time to divide or repot.

FERTILE SOIL AND ABUNDANT MOISTURE INSURE NEOMARICA LONGIFOLIA, *above*, **WILL FLOWER EVEN THROUGH TORRID WEATHER.**

101

NERINE
GUERNSEY LILY

A ship bound for Holland, bearing precious cargo of the Dutch East India Company, wrecked in 1659 in the English Channel. Crates of bulbs that had been loaded in South Africa floated to the beaches of the island of Guernsey. They rooted in the sand and gradually moved inland.

The exotic scarlet flowers, with six recurving petals and prominent stamens, bedazzled the island people, who, in time, established a lucrative business selling "Guernsey lilies" to the London florist trade. The umbels of up to ten flowers, produced on strong, two-foot stems, appear to have been dusted with gold. The islanders assumed since the ship had sailed from the Far East that a flower of such mysterious beauty must have come from Japan. The belief persisted for more than a century until *Nerine sarniensis* was rediscovered growing in its native habitat atop Table Mountain in the Cape Province.

Appropriately, the genus name is derived from Nereis, a mythological sea nymph of Greek legends. (The name is usually pronounced nay-*ree*-nee.) Twenty species are native to South Africa, but few are cultivated. Aside from the fabled Guernsey lily, the best known is *N. bowdenii*, found in the highlands near its cousin.

The magenta pink blossoms of *N. bowdenii* measure three inches across, with the six wavy petals curving back gracefully. They are held in clusters of up to fifteen flowers on straight, two-foot stems over thin, glossy leaves.

Potting occurs in spring, with the necks of the *Nerine* bulbs just above the surface of the soil. The leaves grow throughout the summer in a partially sunny location, and the flower stalks appear and elongate in late summer or fall. The flowers last an exceedingly long time, and in temperate climates the plants are brought inside to finish their fall display. After the foliage has died down, the pots are rested and kept cool and dry; *Nerine* bloom best when crowded so re-potting is put off until the bulbs fairly burst their containers.

AS AUTUMN RETURNS, NERINE BOWDENII **UNFOLDS ITS WAVY PETALS.**

ORNITHOGALUM

CHINCHERINCHEE

Ornithogalum thyrsoides grows wild in the western Cape Province of South Africa, where apparently the breeze rustling through the flowers creates a unique musical noise. The vernacular name chincher-inchee is an attempt to imitate the sound of the peduncles as they rub together, although it sounds more to me like lyrics from *Mary Poppins*. My potted plants of chincherinchee lack any musical inclination that I can detect (perhaps they need a really stiff breeze to rise to the occasion.)

O. thyrsoides has been cultivated since at least the beginning of the eighteenth century and was likely an import to Europe by the Dutch East India Company. It was first called tinkerintees or *viooltjie* (violin) and it appears that the imaginations of eighteen-century plant hunters far outstripped those of most of us today.

Regardless of their musical abilities, chincherinchees make fine, long-blooming pot plants for the summer patio. The green bulbs are planted closely together in deep pots filled with well-draining soil, although they thrive with regular moisture throughout the season. Some gardeners with greenhouses and bright winter gardens grow fine specimens in the winter as well, and cut stems appear in flower shops throughout most of the year.

The blossoms last for a very long time, and many small cup-shaped flowers are closely spaced on the upper third of the leafless spikes growing up to two feet tall above the linear basal foliage The flowers bloom in white with a pale green stripe on the outside of each of the six petals, while some flowers tend toward sulphur yellow, and new hybrids promise clear yellows.

WHEN COLD WEATHER ARRIVES IN TEMPERATE CLIMATES, LATE-BLOOMING AND LONG-LASTING CHINCHERINCHEE, ORNITHOGALUM THYRSOIDES, MUST FINISH BLOOMING INDOORS.

I will forever picture a barber shop when I think of *O. longibracteatum* (formerly *O. caudatum*). When I was a boy, my barber grew an enormous, overcrowded pot of a curious plant. He called it a sea onion, because, I imagined, of the pale green bulbs. I've learned since that it also goes by the folk name pregnant' onion. The "mother bulb" produces offspring under her skin. They swell and as the outer skin peels away, the "babies" drop onto the soil and take root.

It flowers on long, thin spikes shooting into the air on wiry stems, but they are no great floral beauties. The main fascination is the curved, arching leaves—up to five feet long—emanating from those bulbs.

A COLLECTION OF DROUGHT-TOLERANT POTTED PLANTS, *left,* **INCLUDES CHINCHERINCHEE, SILVER** VERBASCUM **'ARCTIC SUMMER', PROSTRATE ROSEMARY, AND** GER-ANIUM MADERENSE **BENEATH A LARGE INDIAN HAWTHORNE,** RHAPHIOLEPIS INDICA. **EASY TO GROW INDOORS OR OUT, A POT OF PREGNANT ONION,** *right,* **IS NEARLY IMMORTAL.**

Oxalis

WOOD SORREL

Oxalis receives the most attention from retailers shortly before St. Patrick's Day, gussied up with green ribbons and leprechaun. The resemblance of their leaves to those of shamrock is responsible, although the plants are not related. Nonetheless, *Oxalis* are often called good luck or four-leaved clover plants.

Oxys, meaning acid, was the Greek name for sorrel, for the taste of the plant's sap. The majority of the many *Oxalis* grow in South America and South Africa, although not all species have bulbous roots. Some are dreaded garden weeds, while others make pretty, easy-care house plants. The leaves are enhanced by delicate flowers.

The red-spotted green leaves of *O. deppei* make it a logical candidate for Irish festivities though the plant is a native of Mexico. Its red or rose pink flowers dangle from ten inch stems. The selected form 'Iron Cross' is distinguished by reddish brown patches at the base of its leaflets.

Clusters of pale pink or white flowers hover above the deep maroon leaves of *O. regnelli* (formerly *O. triangularis*) from South America. The name *O. braziliensis* tells its country of origin. Its showy flowers measure more than an inch

THE HANDSOME, SHAMROCK-SHAPED LEAVES OF OXALIS REGNELLI **MAKE IT A WINNING ACCENT PLANT**, *left*, **OR A LONG-BLOOMING SPECIMEN WITH CLUSTERS OF PASTEL FLOWERS**, *above*.

109

across, and their red color, accented by yellow throats, is set off by a low, four-inch carpet of leaves. Similar *O. crassipes* bears white or pink blossoms. *O. adenophylla* from southern Chile and Argentina often grows in rock gardens, but the dwarf, three-inch-tall plants can be enjoyed in pots as well. Grey-green leaves accent its single flowers striped with deep lavender-pink.

Some species go dormant in very hight heat and should be rested, without water, until autumn. *Oxalis* can be brought indoors and enjoyed during the winter as well.

OXALIS BRAZILIENSIS **FORMS A DENSE CLUMP OF SMALL LEAVES.**

'IRON CROSS' COMPLEMENTS WELL-STAGED POTS OF FLOWERING ANNUALS.

POLIANTHES

TUBEROSE

NO ONE WILL NOTICE IF A FEW STEMS ARE MISSING FROM
THIS WASHTUB OF SINGLE TUBEROSES.

112

The sweet honey-and-vanilla scent of tuberoses made them a precious commodity in sixteenth-century Europe, but there's a bit of a mystery. Although *Polianthes tuberosa* is probably native to Mexico, for none of the other seven species of the genus has ever been found outside that nation, it has never been found in the wild. Some authorities suggest that after centuries of European cultivation—double-flowered forms appeared in the early part of the eighteenth century—that *P. tuberosa* differed so much from its wild characteristics that it was impossible to recognize. Our tuberoses may be the product of centuries of selection from the Mexican wild flower *P. gracilis*.

Polianthes is derived from the Greek *polios*, white, and *anthos*, flower, obviously by a botanist who was not having an inspired day.

So popular was the scent of tuberoses during Victorian times that bulbs were imported on a large scale to England from Italy for growing in glass houses. Percy Shelly, the English poet, settled in Italy in 1818, before heated green-houses were used on a larg scale in his homeland. Perhaps spurring the British interest in the flower, he wrote, of "sweet tuberose, the sweetest flower for scent that blows." Tuberoses were shunned for a good part of this century because too many

people associated their powerful fragrance with funeral bouquets. Armloads of the sweet-scented flowers, displayed at stuffy services, haunt too many mournful memories.

In addition, gardeners in northern climates also had trouble getting the late-season bloomers to flower before frost, and getting them to bloom the next year. The popularity of tuberoses plummeted.

Growing the bulbs in pots solves many problems. As members of the Agave family, tuberoses thrive in heat and sunshine. A clay pot heats up by day and holds warmth during the evening, speeding growth. While moisture is necessary, the narrow basal foliage of tuberoses, up to two feet long, can bake on the terrace or brick wall with little ill effect. Bulbs split after flowering, so it takes an additional year of growth for them to reach flowering size.

The double flowers of 'The Pearl' are set in pairs on stems as tall as thirty inches. Each waxy bud is tinted flesh pink on the outer petals and opens creamy white. The single variety is more to my liking, perhaps because it conveys more of the wild appeal of the original species. As autumn descends on the garden and the first tuberoses open, I transport the pot to the bedroom window. A month of sweet dreams is assured.

SAUROMATUM

VOODOO LILY

Who could resist a plant with such an enticing name? I certainly couldn't. I bought a few plump, six-inch tubers several years ago at the Philadelphia Flower Show and potted them when I came home. I read up on voodoo lily, discovering its proper name *Sauromatum* stems from the Greek *sauros*, meaning lizard, in allusion to the markings on the spathe of its flower. I also found that it is native to the Himalayas and has been cultivated since 1815, sometimes under the less intriguing name monarch-of-the-east.

My windowsills were chock full of blooming bulbs, so I asked my friend Mary Ellen if she had space for a few extra pots. She went home with her *S. venosum* (formerly *S. guttatum*) with the warning that the extraordinarily exotic flowers might have an offensive smell. She called three weeks later. A flower was blooming, a hooded spathe more than a foot high curling back and twisting, revealing an interior of pale green and lavender marbled with chocolate spots. This spathe, like that of a calla lily, surrounds a long central spadix studded with the very tiny true flowers.

THE FASCINATING BUT FETID FLOWERS OF VOODOO LILY ARE FOLLOWED BY GLORIOUS FOLIAGE ON MYSTERIOUSLY MOTTLED STEMS.

"How bad does it smell?" I inquired. "It's fine," she replied, "with just a slight sweet scent." She told me she'd bring it by the next day for me to photograph.

What a difference a day makes. The sweet scent had turned to "Eau d'Roadkill." For fear of tearing the flowers in the wind, Mary Ellen had driven twenty miles with the windows rolled up, no doubt with a horde of flies (who, attracted to the stench, pollinate the flowers) in hot pursuit. She looked a bit green around the gills. We both admired the flowers from a distance on my airy front porch.

After they faded, purple-mottled, eighteen-inch stalks pushed through the soil and unfurled enormous umbrella-like leaves nearly two feet across. Handsome as could be (and thankfully scentless) they sat like an imposing parlor palm indoors until the weather warmed. In a partially shady corner of the patio, the voodoo lily leaves formed an impressive tropical backdrop for tuberous begonias, impatiens, and fuchsias.

The tubers rest in their pots in the cool basement after the leaves have faded in the fall. I start the tubers indoors in May now, late enough so the flowers bloom outdoors, as the plant is worth growing for its foliage alone. Mary Ellen has not volunteered to dabble in voodoo again.

Sprekelia

AZTEC LILY

Of all the exotic bulbs from Mexico, Aztec lily most evokes the mysterious intrigue of a vanished culture. Not that there is any evidence to link the flower directly to the Aztecs, but its form and color would surely have inspired ancient artisans.

J. H. von Sprekelsen of Hamburg, Germany sent the as-yet-unnamed plant to Linnaeus in 1658, and was honored with the genus *Sprekelia* for his effort. The only species of the monotypic genus is *S. formosissima*, which resembles amaryllis.

SPREKELIA FORMOSISSIMA, *top.*
STERNBERGIA LUTEA, *middle.*

Narrow, pointed leaves are produced with or after the solitary, long-lasting flowers, which are borne on smooth stems a foot to eighteen inches high. The crimson blossoms bear six petals arranged into top and bottom sections. Large bulbs often produce more than one flower stem, and crowded bulbs may bloom repeatedly over the summer.

Potted in early spring, the neck of the bulb should protrude above the soil line. Protect *Sprekelia* from afternoon sun. Keep moist except during winter dormancy in a cool, dark location indoors.

TIGRIDIA PAVONIA, *bottom.*

116

STERNBERGIA

GOLDEN CHALICE

Only five species comprise the genus *Sternbergia*, and all are native to the Middle East and the Mediterranean region. Two bloom in spring, but three obstinately bloom in autumn, when gardeners most value their golden crocus-like blossoms. They differ from the genus *Crocus* in one main respect: *Sternbergia* possesses six stamens compared to three for *Crocus*. The flowers of all species are yellow save for white spring-blooming *S. candida*.

The genus honors botanist Count Kaspar Moritz von Sternberg (1761-1838) of Prague. The most commonly grown species, *S. lutea*, is native to the eastern Mediterranean countries, the Caucasus, and Iran. It is among the most appealing of autumn-flowering bulbs, holding its flowers, two inches wide and as long, above the thin, reedy leaves like a golden chalice. The flowers rise six inches high. *S. lutea* is planted in pots in late summer in gritty soil and treated like the autumn-flowering crocus, which make pretty companions.

TIGRIDIA

MEXICAN SHELLFLOWER

It is surprising that a flower named for a tiger would bear spots instead of stripes. Early Spanish botanists, who introduced the flower to Europe late in the eighteenth century, confused the South American spotted jaguar with the Asiatic striped tiger. *Tigridia* is indeed meant to denote a spotted flower. Gardeners have side-stepped the confusion by calling it Mexican shellflower.

The flowers of *T. pavonia* range from vivid red and orange to yellow and white, some with no spots. *Pavonia* means peacocklike and, oddly enough, the flower is known by some as peacock tiger flower. Each flower lasts only a single day, but is replaced each morning for weeks on end in midsummer.

Potted *Tigridia* corms grow best in a deep container placed in a sunny situation, and need attention so that they do not dry out, as well as weekly feeding. At season's end, the corms can be cured and stored like those of gladiolus.

TULBAGHIA

SOCIETY GARLIC

THE ARCHING STEMS AND STRIPED LEAVES OF TULBAGHIA VIOLACEA
'SILVER QUEEN' MAKE IT A YEAR-ROUND ASSET.

While they are not known for their floral fireworks, few plants make such small demands on a gardener as *Tulbaghia*. The genus is native to South Africa, and named for an eighteenth-century governor of the Cape of Good Hope, Ryk Tulbagh. Although it might be easily assumed that *Tulbaghia*, known as society garlic, belongs to the onion family, *Alliacaea*, botanists currently place them in the amaryllis tribe.

The best known species, *T. violacea*, has been grown since the early Victorian period and is a favorite landscape plant in its homeland. Its tuberous roots support thick tufts of grassy leaves topped in summer by stalks carrying umbels of up to twenty flowers. It is sometimes called pink agapanthus, although the small mauve pink flowers bear a more of a resemblance to those of chives, and the leaves smell of chives as well. Native Africans brew a tea from them to relieve headaches, though I can only imagine how it tastes.

The prettiest form of society garlic, sometimes called 'Silver Queen', has variegated leaves, and is pretty throughout the year even while not in bloom. Late in the season *T. fragrans* sports lavender-pink flowers that smell lightly of hyacinths.

VARIEGATED FOLIAGE, INCLUDING THAT OF PINK-FLOWERING TULBAGHIA VIOLACEA **'SILVER QUEEN', TIES TOGETHER BEAUTIFULLY STAGED CONTAINERS.**

ZANTEDESCHIA

SUMMER CALLA LILY

The calla lilies of summer differ from the giant white calla normally grown indoors in late winter, *Z. aethiopica*. Although all species originate in South Africa, the white calla is essentially a winter-flowering bog plant, while *Z. elliottiana* and *Z. rehmannii* bloom in summer in the southern hemisphere.

The rhizomes of the summer bloomers can be planted indoors in late winter. They thrive in an organically rich soil mix kept slightly moist at all times. The juice of the plants marks clothing with a brown stain that defies laundry detergent.

The six inch long spathe of the blossom of *Z. elliottiana* is colored canary yellow and is carried on stalks that can attain three feet in height. The broad leaves appear to have been spattered with metallic silver paint.

Z. rehmannii can be distinguished from other calla lilies by its narrow, pointed leaves. They carry pale green or white spots. The color of its flower spathe varies from vellum white through shades of pink and maroon. The flowers are carried on stems as tall as two feet.

Many selected forms and hybrids expand the color range even further. 'Flame' lives up to its name with orange red flowers, while 'Gem' sports amethyst pink flowers.

ZEPHYRANTHES

ZEPHYR LILY

AMETHYST PINK 'GEM' IS ONE OF THE NEW CALLA LILY HYBRIDS, *left.* **MOST ZEPHYR LILIES, INCLUDING** ZEPHYRANTHES GRANDIFLORA, *above,* **ARE POTTED IN SPRING AND LEFT UNDISTURBED FOR FIVE YEARS OR MORE. THE EXCEPTION IS** Z. ATAMASCO, **WHICH IS POTTED IN OCTOBER.**

Native to the Americas, from Colombia to the southeastern United States, only a handful of species of *Zephyranthes* is often cultivated. The pretty blossoms take both their scientific and common names from the Greek *zephyros*, the west wind. Other folk names include fairy lily and rain lily, for the tendency of the garden-grown flowers to pop up unexpectedly after a rain storm.

Perhaps the fairest of the flowers-of-the-west-wind, *Z. grandiflora* from Guatemala bears rose pink flowers, measuring four inches or more across, on eight inch stems. It is rivaled in beauty by *Z. atamasco*, the swamp lily, which grows wild in many southern states. The species name *atamasco* is a native American word meaning "stained with red" and describes white flowers tinted with pink.

Z. candida from South America saves its display of white flowers until late in the summer or early fall and might easily be mistaken for an autumn-flowering crocus. The blossoms rise on six inch stems over narrow, evergreen leaves.

Bright light and abundant moisture suit them during the growing season. *Z. grandiflora* and *Z. atamasco* lose their leaves in the fall, when watering is reduced, although the pots should not be allowed to go bone dry.

TIME TABLE FOR SUMMER BULBS

TIMING IS APPROXIMATE; TEMPERATURE, HUMIDITY, AND LOCATION INFLUENCE FLOWERING TIME AND DURATION OF FLOWERS.

FLOWER NAMES	WEEKS FROM POTTING TO FLOWERS	TIME TO PLANT	TIME IN BLOOM
Achimenes	8	Feb.–March	2–3 mos.
Acidanthera	14	April–May	2–3 wks.
Agapanthus (from revival)	12	March–April	2–3 mos.
Allium			
capa var. *aggregatum*	—	May	—
schoenoprasum	8	March–April	3–4 wks.
senescens	14	May	2–3 wks.
tuberosum	14	May	3–4 wks.
Alstroemeria	10	March–April	many mos.
Amarcrinum	14	April–May	3–4 wks.
Amaryllis belladonna	9 mos.	Aug.–Sept.	2–3 wks.
Anigozanthos	10	April–May	1–3 mos.
Arisaema	8	Feb.–March	3 wks.
Begonia	10	Feb.–March	3–4 mos.
Belamcanda	14	April–May	2–4 wks.
Caladium	—	April–June	—
Canna	12	March–May	2 mos.
Colchicum	1–3	August	2–3 wks.
Colocasia	—	March–June	—
Crinum	12–16	April–May	3 wks.
Crocosmia	10	April–May	2–4 wks.
Crocus (autumn)	3–5	Aug.–Sept.	2–4 wks.
Curcuma	14	April–May	4–6 wks.
Dahlia	14	April–May	2 mos.
Dicentra			
eximia	8	March–April	3–4 mos.
spectabilis	6	Feb.–March	3–4 wks.

Dietes	8	Sept.–Oct.	many mos.
Erythronium	18–22	Sept.–Oct.	3 wks.
Eucomis	12	April–May	2 mos.
Galtonia	12	April–May	3–4 wks.
Gladiolus	12	April–May	2–4 wks.
Haemanthus	14	March–May	3–5 wks.
Hedychium	14	April–May	6–8 wks.
Hemerocallis	10	March–April	1–2 mos.
Hymenocallis	10	April–May	2–3 wks.
Ipomoea	—	April–June	—
Liatris	14	March–May	3–5 wks.
Lilium			
Asiatic hybrids	10	April–May	3 wks.
Orientals	14–16	April–May	3 wks.
trumpets	12	April–May	3 wks.
Lycoris	10 mos.	Aug.–Sept.	3–4 wks.
Neomarica	12	April–May	1–2 mos.
Nerine	24	March–May	3–4 wks.
Ornithogalum			
arabicum	14	April–May	3–4 wks.
longibracteatum	—	anytime	—
thyrsoides	14	March–May	4–6 wks.
umbellatum	10	Feb.	3–4 wks.
Oxalis	8	anytime	variable
Polianthes	20	April–May	4 wks.
Sauromatum	8	Feb.–April	1–2 wks.
Sprekelia	8	March–April	2–3 wks.
Sternbergia	6	Aug.–Sept.	2–3 wks.
Tigridia	12	March–April	3–5 wks.
Tulbaghia	12	Feb.–April	3–5 wks.
Zantedeschia	8–10	March–April	5–7 wks.
Zephyranthes	16	March–April	3–5 wks.

THE BULB GROWER'S YEAR

(TIMING IS APPROXIMATE DEPENDING ON YOUR REGION. GARDENERS IN WARM AREAS SHOULD PLANT IN THE FIRST MONTH WHERE THE PLANT APPEARS; IN COLD REGIONS SELECT THE LAST MONTH OR THE END OF A MONTH)

JANUARY
◆Enjoy chilled spring bulbs and tender winter-blooming bulbs.
◆Pot: *Begonia, Hippeastrum, Oxalis,* paperwhite *Narcissus, Sprekelia.*
◆Topdress: *Bletilla, Erythronium.*
◆Bring *Clivia* into a warmer, brighter room.

FEBRUARY
◆Enjoy chilled spring bulbs and tender winter-blooming bulbs.
◆Pot (or begin watering those stored in soil in their pots): *Achimenes, Arisaema, Begonia, Canna, Colocasia, Dicentra spectabilis, Sauromatum, Sinningia, Sprekelia, Tritonia, Tulbaghia.*
◆Topdress: *Agapanthus, Amarcrinum, Crinum, Curcuma, Hedychium, Hymenocallis, Neomarica, Nerine, Ornithogalum.*

MARCH
◆Pot: *Achimenes, Agapanthus, Allium schoenoprasum, Alstroemeria, Arisaema, Begonia, Caladium, Canna, Colocasia, Dicentra eximia, D. spectabilis, Eucomis, Gloriosa, Nerine, Sauromatum, Sinningia, Sprekelia, Tigridia, Tulbaghia,* summer *Zantedeschia, Zephyranthes.*

APRIL
◆Pot: *Acidanthera, Alstroemeria, Agapanthus, Amarcrinum, Anigozanthos, Belamcanda, Caladium, Canna, Colocasia, Crinum, Crocosmia, Curcuma, Dahlia, Dicentra eximia, Eucomis, Galtonia, Gladiolus, Gloriosa, Haemanthus, Hedychium, Hemerocallis, Hymenocallis, Ipomoea, Liatris, Lilium, Neomarica, Nerine, Ornithogalum thyrsoides, O. arabicum, Polianthes, Sauromatum, Sprekelia, Tigridia, Tulbaghia,* summer *Zantedeschia.*
◆Continue to water and fertilze spring-flowering bulbs that have finished their show; move pots outdoors.

MAY
◆Pot: *Acidanthera, Allium, Amarcrinum, Anigozanthos, Belamcanda, Canna, Colocasia, Crinum, Crocosmia, Curcuma, Dahlia, Eucomis, Galtonia, Gladiolus, Gloriosa, Haemanthus, Hedychium, Hemerocallis, Hymenocallis, Ipomoea, Liatris, Lilium, Neomarica, Nerine, Ornithogalum thyrsoides, O. arabicum, Polianthes.*
◆Transplant spring bulbs into garden; stop watering those in pots as they go dormant.
◆Transplant *Hippeastrum* into the ground for summer.
◆Move outdoors (when night temperatures remain above 55 to 60° F.): *Begonia, Caladium, Colocasia, Canna, Curcuma, Hedychium; Amaryllis belladonna* (but do not water).
◆Move outdoors to rest in shade (water but do not fertilize): *Clivia, Eucharis, Veltheimia.*
◆Rest: Tender winter bloomers: *Albuca, Allium triquetrum, A. perdulce, Anemone coronaria, Babiana, Bletilla, Bowiea, Cyclamen, Cyrtanthus, Freesia, Ixia, Lachenalia, Phaedranassa, Ranunculus, Sinningia, Sparaxis, Tritonia, Watsonia, Zantedeschia aethiopica.*

JUNE
◆Move outdoors: *Begonia, Caladium, Colocasia, Canna, Curcuma, Gloriosa, Hedychium, Oxalis.*

◆Pot: bulbs listed in May for staggered period of bloom.
◆Store spring-blooming bulbs that were not transplanted into garden.
◆Rest outdoors: *Clivia, Eucharis, Veltheimia*.
◆Fertilize summer bloomers.

JULY
◆Begin to water *Amaryllis belladonna*.
◆Fertlize all bulbs, check for spider mites and slugs.
◆Rest: *Brodieae, Dicentra spectabilis, Sinningia*.

AUGUST
◆Order spring-flowering bulbs.
◆Pot: *Amaryllis belladonna, Cyclamen, Freesia, Lachenalia*; fall bloomers: *Colchicum, Crocus, Lycoris, Sternbergia*.

SEPTEMBER
◆Pot: *Amaryllis belladonna, Dietes, Lycoris*; hardy spring-bloomers; tender winter-bloomers: *Albuca, Allium triquetrum, A. perdulce, Anemone coronaria, Babiana, Bletilla, Bowiea, Cyclamen, Cyrtanthus, Freesia, Gloriosa, Lachenalia, Oxalis, Ranunculus, Veltheimia, Watsonia, Zantedeschia aethiopica*; fall bloomers: *Colchicum, Crocus, Sternbergia*.
◆Increase watering: *Veltheimia*.
◆Heal in pots of (bury in trenches in temperate climates): *Arisaema, Belamcanda, Colchicum, Dicentra, Hemerocallis, Liatris, Lilium*.

OCTOBER
◆Pot: *Hippeastrum*, paperwhite *Narcissus*, pre-cooled *Hyacinth* and *Tulipa, Zephyranthes atamasco*.
◆Rest: *Achimenes, Agapanthus*, summer *Allium, Amarcrinum, Anigozanthos, Begonia, Caladium, Canna, Clivia, Colocasia, Crinum, Crocosmia, Curcuma, Dahlia, Eucomis, Galtonia, Gladiolus, Hedychium, Hymenocallis, Lilium, Neomarica, Sauromatum, Sprekelia, Tigridia*, summer *Zantedeschia*.
◆Bring *Hippeastrum* in from garden after first frost.
◆Grow *Amaryllis belladonna, Haemanthus*, and *Lycoris* foliage indoors.

NOVEMBER
◆Plant *Colchicum, Crocus, Sternbergia* in garden after bloom.
◆Pot: *Gladiolus tristus, Hippeastrum, Homeria, Iris, Ixia, Ledebouria*, paperwhite *Narcissus, Zantedeschia aethiopica*, pre-cooled *Hyacinth and Tulip*.
◆Rest: *Amaryllis belladonna, Nerine, Ornithogalum, Polianthes, Tulbaghia*.

DECEMBER
◆Pot: *Hippeastrum*, paperwhite *Narcissus, Oxalis*.
◆Rest: *Amaryllis belladonna, Haemanthus, Lycoris*.

SOURCES

B & D Lilies
330 P Street
Port Townsend, WA $1
(*Lilium, Alstroemeria, Dahlia*)

Blue Dahlia Gardens
Route 1, Box 20
Hutchinson, MN 55350

The Daffodil Mart
Rt. 3, Box 794
Gloucester, VA 23061 $1
(*Allium, Amaryllis belladonna, Amarcrinum, Colchicum*, autumn *Crocus, Erythronium, Lycoris*)

Dutch Gardens
P.O. Box 200
Adelphia, NJ 07710
(wide selection including *Acidanthera, Agapanthus, Crinum, Crocosmia, Dicentra, Eucomis, Nerine, Oxalis, Tigridia*)

Fairyland Begonia/Lily Garden
1100 Griffith
McKinleyville, CA 95521 $1

Kordonowy Dahlias
P.O. Box 568
Kalama, WA 98625

Logee's Greenhouses
141 North Street
Danielson, CT 06239 $3
(rare tropicals including *Ipomoea* 'Blackie')

McClure & Zimmerman
P.O. Box 368
108 W. Winnebago
Friesland, WI 53935
(wide selection including *Amaryllis belladonna, Belamcanda, Colchicum, Erythronium, Lycoris, Ornithogalum, Sternbergia*)

Mt. Hood Lilies
15361 SE Bluff Road
P.O. Box 1314
Sandy, Oregon 97055

Park Seed Co.
Cokesbury Road
Greenwood, SC 29647-0001
(summer exotics including *Achimenes, Caladium, Sprekelia, Zantedeschia*)

Pleasant Valley Glads
P.O. Box 494
Agawam, MA 01001

Smith & Hawken
25 Corte Madera
Mill Valley, CA 94941
(specialty bulbs and containers)

Spaulding Bulb Farm
1811 Howey Road
Sebring, FL 33870
(*Caladium*)

Alex Summerville
R.D. 1, Box 449
Glassboro, NJ 08028
(*Gladiolus*)

Swan Island Dahlias
Box 700
Canby, OR 97013 $3

TyTy Plantation
Box 159
TyTy, GA 31795 $1
(exotics including *Canna, Colocasia, Crinum, Hedychium*)

K. Van Bourgondien & Sons Inc.
P.O. Box 1000
245 Farmingdale Road, Rt. 109
Babylon, NY 11702-0598
(many summer exotics including *Achimenes, Acidanthera, Haemanthus, Hymenocallis, Lycoris, Polianthes, Zephyranthes*)

White Flower Farm
Litchfield, CT 0679-0050
(exotics including *Amarcrinum*)

INDEX

Page numbers set as italics denote the placement of illustrative photographs.